IRPP

Founded in 1972, the Institute for Research on Public Policy is an independent, national, non-profit organization. Its mission is to improve public policy in Canada by promoting and contributing to a policy process that is more broadly based, informed and effective.

In pursuit of this mission, the IRPP

- identifies significant public policy questions that will confront Canada in the longer term future and undertakes independent research into these questions;

- promotes wide dissemination of key results from its own and other research activities;

- encourages non-partisan discussion and criticism of public policy issues in a manner which elicits broad participation from all sectors and regions of Canadian society and links research with processes of social learning and policy formation.

The IRPP's independence is assured by an endowment fund, to which federal and provincial governments and the private sector have contributed.

Créé en 1972, l'Institut de recherche en poli- *25*
tiques publiques est un organisme national et
indépendant à but non lucratif.

L'IRPP a pour mission de favoriser le dévelop-
pement de la pensée politique au Canada par
son appui et son apport à un processus élargi,
plus éclairé et plus efficace d'élaboration et
d'expression des politiques publiques.

Dans le cadre de cette mission, l'IRPP a
pour mandat :

- d'identifier les questions politiques aux-
  quelles le Canada sera confronté dans
  l'avenir et d'entreprendre des recherches
  indépendantes à leur sujet;

- de favoriser une large diffusion des résul-
  tats les plus importants de ses propres
  recherches et de celles des autres sur
  ces questions;

- de promouvoir une analyse et une discussion objectives des questions politiques
  de manière à faire participer activement
  au débat public tous les secteurs de la
  société canadienne et toutes les régions
  du pays, et à rattacher la recherche à
  l'évolution sociale et à l'élaboration de
  politiques.

L'indépendance de l'IRPP est assurée par les
revenus d'un fonds de dotation auquel ont
souscrit les gouvernements fédéral et provin-
ciaux, ainsi que le secteur privé.

INSTITUTE FOR RESEARCH ON PUBLIC POLICY

INSTITUT DE RECHERCHE EN POLITIQUES PUBLIQUES

reforming
federal-
provincial
fiscal arrangements

TOWARD SUSTAINABLE FEDERALISM

BY
PAUL A. R. HOBSON AND FRANCE ST-HILAIRE

IRPP

Printed in Canada

Bibliothèque nationale du Québec
Dépôt légal 1994

Canadian Cataloguing in Publication Data

Hobson, Paul A. R. (Paul Alexander Robert), 1953-
Toward sustainable federalism: reforming federal-provincial fiscal arrangements

Includes bibliographical references.

ISBN 0-88645-153-1

1. Federal-provincial fiscal relations—Canada.
I. St-Hilaire, France II. Institute for Research on Public Policy. III. Title.

HJ795.A1H63 1993   336.3'43271   C94-900067-1

Marye Bos
Director of Publications, IRPP

Copy Editor
Mathew Horsman

Design and Production
Ric Little and Barbara Rosenstein

Cover Illustration
Barbara Rosenstein

Tables and Figures
Michel Leblanc

Published by
The Institute for Research on Public Policy (IRPP)
L'Institut de recherche en politiques publiques
1470 Peel Street, Suite 200
Montreal, Quebec H3A 1T1

Distributed by
Renouf Publishing Co. Ltd.
1294 Algoma Road
Ottawa, Ontario K1B 3W8
For orders, call 613-741-4333

contents

foreword

Federal-provincial fiscal arrangements are under review at a critical time for Canada. Growing debt, large deficits and the increasing costs of social programs are putting intense pressures on the already delicate balance between the federal and provincial governments. Reform is necessary if our system of fiscal federalism is to survive. Hard choices must be made — not only about the mechanisms of fiscal transfers but about the policy objectives these transfers are designed to achieve.

The Institute for Research on Public Policy has taken a particular interest in the subject of fiscal federalism, viewing it as one of the most important topics on the public policy agenda. Transfers are, to a degree, the "glue" of our decentralized federal system. Reforming the existing framework will be key to ensuring the viability of the Canadian union.

Much more than the state of federal-provincial relations is at stake. Transfers are an integral part of the financing of Canadian health care, education and income security programs. As a consequence, fundamental questions must be answered if the reform process is to succeed. Chief among the challenges will be determining the extent to which our current social programs are viable, even in the short term. How much can we afford to spend on health care, and what should our priorities be? How can Canadian education be improved to better prepare the labour force for jobs in the new economy? How can we make the income security system more effective in confronting the problems of the unemployed?

First and foremost, a balance must be struck between the roles of the federal and provincial governments in the financing and delivery of national social programs. Any new arrangements must be flexible, to allow governments to adjust to changing economic circumstances, now and in the future. Most critically in the short term, provinces must have access to adequate levels of financing in order to provide the services for which they are responsible.

In the pages that follow, Paul Hobson and France St-Hilaire trace the history of federal-provincial fiscal arrangements, determine the nature of the pressures now being brought to bear, and propose solutions to the acute problems that jeopardize two of Canada's most important transfer programs, EPF and CAP. Their proposals constitute one possible step on the way toward sustainable fiscal federalism.

In publishing this monograph, IRPP hopes to help focus and advance the current debate on federal-provincial fiscal relations. Informed analysis and practical policy advice are required if we are to embark on a process of meaningful reform.

Monique Jérôme-Forget
President, IRPP

preface

We began discussing the practice of fiscal federalism during the early part of 1993, with the failed Charlottetown Accord as a backdrop and the debt/deficit crisis waiting in the wings, soon to be centre stage. Restructuring federal-provincial fiscal relations is now essential, certainly long overdue, if Canadian-style federalism is to be sustained. We remain of the view, however, that reforming federal-provincial fiscal relations can be done in a manner consistent with the principles of fiscal equity and fiscal efficiency that have characterized the practice of fiscal federalism in Canada since Confederation. To this end, we offer our proposals in the hope that the next act will move the debate forward to a critical evaluation of the various reform options now being considered.

Our ideas were strongly influenced, in their infancy, by discussions with Ken Norrie and Robin Boadway. We have benefitted as well from informal discussions at IRPP with officials from various federal and provincial ministries. We wish to express our gratitude to Robin Boadway, Monique Jérôme-Forget, David Milne, André Raynauld, Russ Robinson and Leslie Seidle for their insightful comments on earlier drafts of the manuscript. Our copy editor was Mathew Horsman, to whom we are indebted for sound advice and encouragement. We also owe special thanks to Liz Reynolds for research assistance and to Michel Leblanc, who helped us with data gathering and who prepared the graphs and figures.

We are, of course, grateful to IRPP, which sponsored the research and writing process, and in particular to Monique Jérôme-Forget, its president. IRPP staff, particularly Marye Bos, director of publications, provided valued support.

We wish to dedicate this work to our children — Edey, Elizabeth, Elyse, Jane and Nicolas. We do so not only to acknowledge that completing a project such as this inevitably takes its toll on family life, but also because we recognize that the sort of structural change now occurring in Canada has the potential to alter fundamentally the character of the country they will inherit. None of us involved in policy debate should take such responsibility lightly.

Paul A. R. Hobson
France St-Hilaire

one

a case of uneasy alliances

Introduction

Much has been said and written about the considerable achievements of fiscal federalism in Canada. For the most part, praise is well deserved. As we know, the system has been instrumental in laying the groundwork for much of the country's social policy, particularly in the areas of health care, social assistance and post-secondary education. Implementing national programs in these areas of provincial jurisdiction required a large measure of federal-provincial partnership. At the same time, ensuring consistency with fundamental equity objectives meant that the fiscal partnership had to incorporate some redistributive features. In hindsight, the practice of fiscal federalism was relatively straightforward when the issues consisted primarily of implementing grand designs — national health care, comprehensive social assistance and accessible education — in an environment of economic growth and prosperity. As we are now painfully aware, the real challenges lay ahead.

The economic and fiscal environment has changed markedly since the major social programs were put in place. Faced with unprecedented levels of debt and deficit, high unemployment and relatively weak growth prospects, governments are having to reassess all social spending both in terms of effectiveness and sustainability. Measures taken by the federal

government since the mid-1980s to control expenditures are already having a significant impact. Social programs are being affected both directly
through budget cuts in federal programs and indirectly via controls
placed on the growth of transfers to the provinces. These deficit-reducing
efforts have been interpreted by some as, effectively, a withdrawal of federal participation in social policy and have created some uncertainties
concerning the future of national social programs. They have also exacerbated tensions in federal-provincial relations. More significantly, perhaps,
fiscal arrangements that had been the "financial instrument" of federal-
provincial cooperation in social policy[1] have become a stumbling block in
the process of redefining the respective roles of governments in the financing and delivery of social programs — a redefinition that is now recognized as necessary if we are to meet the still valid social objectives set
decades ago.

The three major federal-provincial transfer programs — Equalization,
Established Programs Financing (EPF) and the Canada Assistance Plan
(CAP) — as well as the Tax Collection Agreements, under which Ottawa
collects income taxes on behalf of participating provinces, are all presently under review. This process, which is meant to be completed by the end
of the 1993-94 fiscal year, will be influenced, no doubt, by the issues
brought to the fore in the latest round of constitutional negotiations.[2] The
proposals for constitutional amendment that emerged from Charlottetown
pertaining to federal-provincial arrangements are an indication of the
problems at hand. For instance, much discussion took place on the need
to introduce a social charter, along with constitutional guarantees to pro-
tect federal-provincial cost-sharing agreements against the sort of unilateral federal action that has hampered federal-provincial fiscal relations in
recent years. At the same time, there was also considerable effort devoted
to developing mechanisms aimed at limiting the federal spending power
and to specifying opting-out provisions. However, it is the ongoing federal
preoccupation with fiscal restraint and the provinces' own budgetary difficulties that will, clearly, set the tone of these negotiations.

All the same, the issues at stake go far beyond budgetary concerns. In
a federal system, intergovernmental fiscal arrangements determine how
services are provided by various levels of government and who pays for
them; they involve the delimitation of the respective roles of each level of

government, the level and means of redistribution, as well as the contentious issue of national standards and their role in promoting efficiency in the economic union. In that sense, fiscal federalism is a delicate balancing act that affects a number of key policy objectives, and its design has broad-ranging implications for the future of the federation.

Our intent is to explore changes in the federal-provincial fiscal arrangements that are consistent with the principles of fiscal equity and fiscal efficiency — principles that have characterized the practice of fiscal federalism in Canada since Confederation. It is our view that these key principles can and should be preserved, notwithstanding the present preoccupation of governments with deficit reduction. It is also the case, however, that federal-provincial fiscal arrangements must be adapted to the new policy imperatives that are emerging as Canada's welfare state is redefined.

National Equity and the Role of Governments

The evolution of federal-provincial fiscal arrangements over the post-war years has been directly related to the notion of Canada as a federal system committed to the pursuit of national equity as a principal policy goal. Broadly speaking, this goal was given constitutional recognition in section 36, The Constitution Act, 1982, entitled "Equalization and Regional Disparities." Part 1 commits both levels of government to:

(a) [promote] equal opportunities for the well-being of Canadians;

(b) [further] economic development to reduce disparity in opportunities; and

(c) [provide] essential public services of reasonable quality to all Canadians.

Part 2 commits the federal government to:

the principle of making equalization payments to ensure that provincial governments have sufficient revenues to provide reasonably comparable levels of public services at reasonably comparable levels of taxation.

Yet the division of powers and responsibilities as laid out in The Constitution Act, 1867, assigns broad jurisdiction to the provinces in "matters of a local or private nature." Included in this broad category are health care, social assistance and social services. In addition, exclusive legislative jurisdiction is assigned to the provinces in the key areas of education and hospitals. The federal government was assigned responsibility for unemployment insurance in 1940, following a constitutional amendment.

Nonetheless, there has been considerable federal involvement in the development of provincially operated social programs, primarily through the use of the spending power. This has traditionally been justified on the grounds that the federal government has the broad power to make expenditures that are in the "public" and/or "national" interest. In addition, the Constitution Act, 1982 provides explicit grounds for federal spending in the social policy field, not only under the terms of section 36 but also under the Charter of Rights and Freedoms, which enshrined mobility and equality rights of persons. Since the federal government cannot legislate in areas such as education, health care and social assistance — areas that have significant equity dimensions — it can only fulfil its mandate through the use of various transfer programs, both to individuals and to provincial governments.

The Major Federal-Provincial Transfer Programs

A crucial aspect of the practice of fiscal federalism in Canada has been the retention of sufficient federal control over the personal and corporate income tax fields to enable the central government to maintain a significant presence in provincial finances through the major fiscal transfer programs. For the 1992-93 fiscal year, the federal Department of Finance estimates that 27.2 percent of provincial gross revenues can be attributed to the major fiscal transfer programs. This figure represents a total of $35.5 billion, of which $24.2 billion is in the form of cash transfers, representing almost 22 percent of federal program expenditures.

Through the fiscal equalization program, the federal government makes unconditional revenue transfers to the designated have-not provinces to offset fiscal disparities, ostensibly enabling these provinces to fund levels of services comparable to those of other provinces without resorting to unduly high levels of taxation. Under EPF, the federal government provides equal per-capita transfers to the provinces in respect of health care and post-secondary education expenditures. Under the CAP agreements, the federal government shares with the provinces the cost of eligible provincial expenditures for social assistance and social services. As shown in figure 1, EPF, at $20.8 billion, is by far the largest of these three programs, followed by Equalization at $8.4 billion and CAP at $7.2 billion.

figure 1

Federal Transfers to Provinces, 1992-93

Total=$39.2 billion*

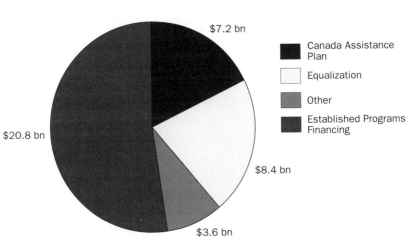

* Equalization associated with tax transfers under EPF is included in both EPF and Equalization. The transfer total has been adjusted to avoid double-counting the associated Equalization.

Source: Department of Finance (1992).

The relative importance of these fiscal transfers as a percentage of revenues varies significantly across provinces, ranging from 44 percent in Newfoundland to only 20 percent in Alberta. As shown in figure 2, there is a marked difference between those provinces that are recipients of equalization payments — Newfoundland, Prince Edward Island, Nova

Scotia, New Brunswick, Quebec, Manitoba and Saskatchewan — and the remaining three provinces in terms of their reliance on federal transfers.

figure 2

Major Federal Transfers as a Share of Provincial Revenues
1992-93

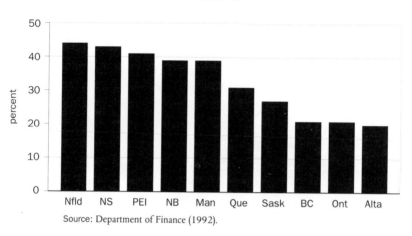

Source: Department of Finance (1992).

Current Status

Either directly or indirectly, each of the fiscal transfer programs has been affected by the strained fiscal environment of the 1990s. Per-capita entitlements under EPF have been subject to a five-year freeze since 1990-91. Also for a five-year period beginning in 1990-91, annual growth in entitlements under CAP in British Columbia, Alberta, and Ontario — the three have provinces — has been subjected to a five percent ceiling (the so-called cap on CAP). Growth in entitlements under fiscal equalization has also been restrained by means of a ceiling provision put in place in 1982. This provision, which limits the rate of growth of equalization transfers to the rate of growth of GDP over a designated base year, had an impact on provincial revenues each year between 1988-89 and 1991-92.

Federal deficit-cutting measures, insofar as they affect intergovernmental transfer payments, have inevitably had serious budgetary implications for the provinces. According to estimates produced by the Ontario government[3], the cumulative revenue loss since 1982-83 for all provinces resulting from federal expenditure controls on the major transfer programs amounts to $40.8 billion. In 1992-93 alone, it is estimated that transfers will be 21 percent lower than they would have been in the absence of federal expenditure controls — a $9.4 billion revenue shortfall. There has been an on-going debate between the federal government and the provinces as to the legitimacy of estimates such as these. The issues involve whether intergovernmental transfers have been and should be treated like any other budget item in the context of a deficit reduction program and whether the federal government has been "offloading" part of its deficit to the provinces. Whatever the case may be, the consequence of the federal measures is apparent in the dramatic increase in net borrowing on the part of provincial governments in recent years (from $1.5 billion in 1989 to $25.7 billion in 1992).

This has also led to a situation in which all provinces — the haves and the have-nots — are financing an increasing share of their expenditures out of own-source revenues. The implications are straightforward when it comes to provincial budget decisions. With the marginal cost of social program expenditures rising for all provinces, the choice is between raising additional revenues or cutting services, or a combination of both.

Furthermore, the relative cost increases have been uneven across provinces. For instance, the erosion of cash transfers under EPF resulting from the freeze on per-capita entitlements means that provinces seeking to replace lost revenues from own-sources must do so while facing radically different fiscal capacities, particularly in the presence of the ceiling on equalization. By the same token, the five percent growth ceiling imposed on CAP transfers to the have provinces has meant that, beyond this ceiling, social assistance expenditures incurred in those provinces are no longer eligible for cost sharing.

The situation is not likely to improve. EPF is delivered through a combination of so-called tax transfers and residual cash transfers. With the freeze on per-capita entitlements, there has been a precipitous decline in the residual cash component, raising concerns that the program will cease to be an equal per-capita transfer. Moreover, with the gradual elimination of the cash transfer, the federal government is seen to be losing its leverage over the provinces in applying the provisions of the Canada Health Care Act. Projected increases in provincial expenditures on social assistance will place further pressures on the future of cost sharing under CAP. Finally, the impact of the growth ceiling on equalization[4] is likely to gain importance as the provinces respond to restrictions in the growth in EPF and CAP transfers by imposing higher provincial tax rates. As fiscal capacities differ so significantly across provinces, the ability of individual provinces to compensate for reductions in federal transfers varies accordingly. The capacity of the have-not provinces to continue to provide reasonably comparable levels of public services without resorting to excessive taxation cannot be sustained in such an environment. It is our view that this could seriously compromise the application of the principle of fiscal equity in the Canadian federation.

The provinces, of course, have not been unaware of the fiscal consequences of federal expenditure control programs. The following citation taken from the Western Finance Ministers' Report (prepared at the behest of the Western Premiers) illustrates some of their concerns:

Adequacy and affordability have been considered only in relation to the federal need to reduce expenditure growth — the dollar commitments provinces have to make to maintain costly social programs have been ignored. Flexibility, efficiency, stability and predictability, if considered at all, have been considered in federal terms. For the provinces, fiscal relations through the decade have been marred by inflexibility, inefficiency, instability and unpredictability. Accountability to the public has been destroyed in a "numbers war" between the federal and provincial governments. Lower fiscal capacity and the equalization ceiling make the equalization-recipient provinces especially vulnerable to cuts in other federal programs and transfers which shift responsibilities to the provinces. In the end, the fundamental partnership among the governments in Canada has been severely damaged.[5]

Clearly, individual provinces' response to these problems varies according to their reliance on federal transfers as a source of revenue. Recent attempts to strengthen the federal commitment to making equalization payments and to obtain constitutional protection for intergovernmental agreements[6] received considerable support. However, there is also increasing pressure in the have provinces for a greater degree of fiscal autonomy. Some provinces have actively sought a further transfer of income tax room to provincial governments as a means of disentangling federal and provincial roles in financing programs delivered by the provinces. Although federal spending in provincial areas of jurisdiction does not interfere with provincial legislative authority, some provinces have long maintained that the conditions and other constraints associated with federal transfers are limiting their ability to implement the policy reforms that may be required. Meanwhile, there is considerable concern that the perceived discriminatory treatment of the have provinces as a result of the implementation of the cap on CAP could ultimately erode the commitment in those provinces to the principle of revenue sharing through the fiscal arrangements. As things stand, the fiscal partnership between the federal government and the provinces could be described as, at best, an "uneasy alliance."[7]

Constitutional guarantees, however, do not seem to us to provide a viable solution to the problem. Rather, it is our view that federal-provincial fiscal relations have reached a plateau. A new approach is required that will facilitate rather than impede the adjustments we are now facing in the area of social policy. Just as was the case with the design of fiscal transfers almost three decades ago, the new arrangements will need to reflect contemporary economic realities, the expenditure responsibilities of each level of government and the policy objectives at hand. At a time when accountability, efficiency[8] and fiscal restraint are the order of the day, the true test of fiscal federalism will rest in the degree to which we are able to reform the system while also remaining committed to the fundamental economic principle of equity.

Outline of the Study

In what follows, we focus on the issues underlying the reform of two of the major fiscal transfer programs, EPF and CAP, and provide some specific alternatives. As backdrop to our analysis, we first describe the principles and concepts underlying federal-provincial fiscal arrangements. In chapter 2, two key concepts of fiscal federalism, fiscal equity and fiscal efficiency, are introduced, followed by a discussion of horizontal and vertical fiscal imbalance in federal systems of government and the related issues of accountability and transparency. We conclude the chapter with a description of the fiscal equalization program. Equalization is often referred to as the "glue of federalism." It has even been proposed by some observers that the current fiscal "quagmire" could be avoided simply by eliminating all specific-purpose transfers and maintaining only an enriched equalization program. We do not subscribe to this view. To explain why, we consider what is achieved through equalization and what is not. We also describe the links between equalization and the two other major transfer programs.

In chapter 3, we look at the factors that prompted the shift to block funding of established programs with the introduction of EPF in 1977. Although this appeared to represent a significant change in the nature of federal-provincial fiscal arrangements, we argue that EPF constituted, in fact, a further step in the gradual devolution of income tax room from the federal government to the provinces over the post-war period.

Unlike such previous transfers, however, the number of tax points associated with the effective transfer of tax room under EPF has been eroded in the last decade. This erosion stems both from the formula that was adopted to calculate growth in per-capita EPF entitlements and from a series of federal measures implemented thereafter to further restrict the growth of EPF transfers. It is our view that the devolution of tax room to the provinces with respect to the established programs remains as unfinished business on the federal-provincial fiscal agenda, and that the existing residual cash transfer to the provinces should be converted into a tax abatement with a fixed percentage of federal income tax revenues earmarked for EPF. The yield from this abatement would form the basis for a system of interprovincial revenue sharing. This would accomplish a complete fiscal disentanglement in funding programs included under EPF (the federal government would, in effect, be collecting revenues on behalf of the provinces) and halt the erosion in the value of the implicit number of EPF tax points under the current system.

The policy issues associated with CAP are fundamentally different from those of EPF. CAP involves the provision of income support to needy individuals, and as such is an integral part of the income security system. As is described in chapter 4, this is primarily why CAP remains largely unchanged from its original design, despite its long-recognized inadequacies. For more than twenty years, beginning with the Social Security Review in 1973, there have been calls for a comprehensive reform of income security programs. The same factors that prevented reform initiatives in the past continue to stand in the way today. These have to do mainly with the entanglement of federal-provincial responsibilities in the area of income redistribution and with funding issues, in particular the definition of appropriate fiscal arrangements. The tinkering approach, however, appears to have run its course. The severity of the problems experienced in almost all provinces with respect to social assistance is evidence of this. The difficulties posed by the rising number of unemployed employables who are resorting to welfare and the resulting escalation in social assistance expenditures are such that a complete recasting of the role of social assistance is now inevitable.

CAP will therefore need to be reassessed within the context of a fundamental review of the income security system. There has been a dramatic change in the social assistance clientele in the last decade and this has significant implications for the redesign and financing of CAP programs. In particular, provinces will need greater flexibility to implement the required "active" income support measures. This will probably involve improving the employability enhancement aspects of social services as well as developing appropriate work incentive measures. Moreover, provinces should have greater flexibility under the Tax Collection Agreements to implement and integrate income security measures through the tax system.

Given the federal role in income redistribution and the fact that the demand for social assistance is increasingly tied to economic cycles, we feel there is a strong case for maintaining some form of cost-sharing arrangement for social assistance and social services programs. However, it is clear that the size of transfers in this area should be determined on the basis of relative need rather than ability to spend. The system we propose would not only reflect the counter-cyclical nature of social assistance expenditures but would also take into account differences in economic circumstances across provinces. Specifically, we argue that CAP transfers should be fully equalized for differences in need relative to the national average and we propose a cost-sharing scheme through which this could be accomplished.

The concluding chapter provides a summary of our main arguments and proposals. Underlying our recommendations is a common theme: the need for a renewed commitment to the principle of Canada as a sharing community[9] but one where greater reliance is placed on interprovincial revenue sharing as a means to achieve this. Moreover, we argue that much of the tension underlying federal-provincial fiscal relations in Canada at present can be alleviated within the framework of the existing fiscal arrangements; it is not necessary to reinvent Canadian fiscal federalism. Rather, we are of the view that the time has come to take an evolutionary step forward.

two

fiscal federalism: principles and framework

Over the post-war period, Canada has developed a fairly complex and interrelated tax and transfer structure that has enabled the pursuit of a number of broad policy objectives. On the revenue side, fiscal federalism entails the administration and collection of personal and corporate income taxes by the federal government, both on its own behalf and that of the provinces with which it has Tax Collection Agreements. On the expenditure side, there exists a series of intergovernmental transfers through which significant amounts of tax revenues are redistributed to the provinces. The system, as it has evolved, offers a number of important advantages, not least those associated with harmonized and centralized tax collection and decentralized service delivery. It also defines the way and the extent to which governments can address known market inefficiencies and inequities. As such, federal-provincial fiscal arrangements have become a key building block from which other patterns of taxation and expenditure derive, both at the federal and provincial levels. For these reasons, we strongly support the view recently expressed by Boadway regarding the upcoming review of federal-provincial fiscal arrangements: "A precondition for deciding on a course of action for renewing the fiscal arrangements is a clear idea of the objectives they are intended to fulfil."[10]

Fiscal Equity and Efficiency

The principle of fiscal equity holds that individuals who are otherwise equally well off ought to be treated equally under the fiscal systems of their respective provinces as well as under the federal fiscal system. Fiscal systems comprise both the expenditure activities of governments — such as provision of health care and education, as well as personal transfers such as welfare payments — and the taxes used to finance those activities. So-called Net Fiscal Benefits (NFBs) represent, at the level of the individual, the difference between benefits received from government expenditures and taxes paid.

NFBs arising from provincial fiscal systems may differ among individuals depending on their income. For example, equal per-capita expenditures financed through proportional income taxes will generate different levels of NFBs for different individuals. The value of these will be inversely related to income, declining as income rises and becoming negative for those with above-average incomes. By contrast, expenditures that are financed through benefit-related taxes — that is, taxes that vary according to benefits received — would generate no NFBs. In short, differences in NFBs among individuals in any province can arise from the redistributive nature of provincial budgets. However, when considered in the aggregate, these differences cancel out.

It is differences in NFBs accruing to otherwise equally well-off individuals who reside in different provinces that give rise to the problem of fiscal inequity. NFBs may differ across provinces for a variety of reasons. Principal among these is income disparities — as measured by differences in average incomes — across provinces. For example, a uniform proportional provincial income tax used to finance equal per-capita public expenditures will result in lower NFBs accruing to individuals who happen to be residents of provinces with below-average incomes compared to individuals with the same level of income living in wealthier provinces.

Many of the services provided by the provincial public sector — including health care and education — can be characterized as publicly provided private goods. The principal justification for public sector provision in this regard is that expenditure programs, as well as taxes and transfers, have a potentially significant role to play in the attainment of income redistribution goals. If such services are thought of as equal per-capita expenditures, financed through proportional income taxes, they create positive NFBs for those with below-average incomes and negative NFBs for those with above-average incomes. By the same token, income transfers through social assistance, financed through proportional income taxes, confer positive NFBs on recipients and negative NFBs on all others, the negative NFBs becoming increasingly larger as income rises. The important point, however, is that, if average incomes differ across provinces, NFBs will differ for individuals with the same level of income who reside in different provinces; those who are resident in provinces with below-average incomes will receive lower NFBs, thus violating the principle of fiscal equity.

Since NFB differentials are most pertinent to our discussion, it is worth pursuing the argument further. In excess of 60 percent of provincial expenditures are in the key program areas of education, health care and social assistance. If these services are to be provided at a comparable level per capita across provinces, then there is a case for equalizing fully the per-capita revenues used to finance them. Full equalization of per-capita revenues could be achieved through the centralized collection of income taxes earmarked for these program areas, with equal per-capita redistribution across provinces. In this case, there would need to be an appropriate division of income tax room between the federal government and the provinces. Equivalently, provinces could pool a portion of income tax revenues and redistribute these among themselves on an equal per-capita basis. In this case, the federal government might simply serve the role of coordinating interprovincial revenue pooling by collecting income taxes explicitly on behalf of the provinces and distributing revenues on an equal per-capita basis.

A second source of interprovincial NFB differentials is that associated with differences in access to certain revenue sources such as natural resource royalties. Provinces with relatively high per-capita yields from resource royalties are able to confer correspondingly high NFBs on their residents. This case has received considerable attention in the Canadian context due to the fact that natural resource wealth varies significantly by region.

Finally, interprovincial NFB differentials may also result from differences in preferences for redistribution across provinces. For example, provinces that finance a given level of per-capita spending through relatively more progressive tax systems will cause individuals at the lower end of the income distribution to obtain relatively higher levels of NFBs and those at the upper end of the income distribution to obtain relatively low levels of NFBs compared with their respective counterparts in other provinces.

Differences in NFBs across provinces, therefore, imply that otherwise identical individuals are treated differently based solely on their province of residence. Put another way, the activities of the provincial public sector may result in a significant degree of horizontal inequity across provinces. The presence of NFB differentials across provinces also implies that the federal fiscal structure will be horizontally inequitable. The main reason for this is that individuals are taxed based on their private income (wages, etc.) rather than on their comprehensive income inclusive of NFBs. Thus, a uniform proportional income tax levied by the federal government, for example, would result in individuals with the same level of comprehensive income paying different amounts of tax, according to the level of NFBs generated in their home province. More specifically, individuals in provinces with relatively high levels of NFBs will end up paying less in federal taxes (because NFBs are not included in the tax base). Once again, then, fiscal equity requires that NFBs be equalized across provinces. Note that correcting for differences in NFBs induced through provincial budgets will automatically correct for this source of fiscal inequity associated with the federal fiscal structure.[11]

Finally, differences in NFBs across provinces may give rise to inefficient migration flows that constitute a source of fiscal inefficiency. (By this we mean migration patterns motivated by differences in NFBs, rather than productivity considerations as indicated by wage differentials.) Thus, relatively high NFBs in some provinces may result in excessive immigration, driving down wage rates until comprehensive incomes — wages plus NFBs — are equalized across provinces for otherwise similar individuals. Yet, an efficient allocation of labour across provinces would require that migration occur until wage rates, not comprehensive incomes, are equal.[12] Therefore, efficiency considerations would dictate that NFBs be fully equalized across provinces.

Vertical and Horizontal Fiscal Balance

One of the central issues underlying fiscal arrangements is that of fiscal balance, or, more to the point, fiscal imbalance. Horizontal fiscal balance refers to a province's fiscal capacity relative to that of other provinces. One way of measuring a province's fiscal capacity is to estimate, for a set of representative tax bases, the potential per-capita revenue yield based on standardized tax rates and bases. The presence of horizontal imbalance is apparent when the same "tax effort" generates different levels of revenues across provinces, due to the effect of differing economic circumstances on various tax bases (such as personal income or retail sales). Differences in access to certain revenue sources, such as natural resource royalties, can also explain differences in fiscal capacity. These differences give rise to fiscal inequity and potential fiscal inefficiency. One purpose of fiscal equalization, therefore, is to correct for such horizontal fiscal imbalances within the federation.

Vertical fiscal balance, on the other hand, refers to the degree to which each level of government's access to fiscal resources matches its expenditure responsibilities. The notion of vertical balance is often associated with the concept of fiscal responsibility, the view being that it is preferable for each level of government to be responsible for collecting the revenues it spends.

There are a number of reasons why vertical imbalance may be justified in federal fiscal systems. For example, where equalization is operated as a gross scheme — one that is centrally funded — vertical imbalance between the federal government and the provinces will be required to enable the federal government to finance the program. Additional access to fiscal resources by the central government may also be necessary to implement specific-purpose grants designed to correct for inefficiencies in the provision of provincially supplied services — inefficiencies that can arise when the benefits related to such expenditures spill over into other provinces. For example, this argument has been made in the case of education, where provinces may not get the full benefit of their expenditures, and thus would be inclined to "underspend." Vertical imbalance may also be justifiable — although, no doubt, contentious — when a federal government uses cash transfers to provinces in order to promote the development of national social programs or to enforce national standards in designated program areas, for example health care. However, such objectives have to be weighed against the need for provinces to have both a certain degree of autonomy in establishing programs that reflect particular regional preferences and priorities as well as flexibility in implementing changes in program delivery in response to evolving policy requirements. Finally, where tax harmonization is seen as desirable, it may prove cost effective to centralize revenue collection at the federal level, and institute a system of unconditional transfers to the provinces. These could be on an equalized basis or not.

A significant issue in fiscal federalism is, therefore, determining the appropriate degree of vertical fiscal imbalance. This obviously involves tradeoffs among objectives and, more importantly, considerable flexibility in responding to changing circumstances. This point was emphasized by the 1981 Parliamentary Task Force on Federal-Provincial Fiscal Arrangements (the Breau Report), which concluded that: "The allocation of revenues between the two orders of government must be reviewed at regular intervals, because it must be made to correspond with the allocation of responsibilities, which itself tends to change over time."[13]

The extent of changes in the relative importance of both levels of government since 1950 is illustrated in table 1. The downward trend in federal-provincial spending ratios reflects the increasing importance of provincial expenditures, particularly in the areas of health, education and welfare. The same pattern holds on the revenue side, although, in this case, the federal government has maintained a dominant presence. These ratios can be seen as indicators of decentralization and flexibility. Revenue and expenditure projections reported by the Economic Council in its 1991 annual report[14] suggest that the provincial governments will be under increasing pressure to raise additional tax revenues to meet their expenditure requirements over the next decade. Meanwhile, corresponding projections for the federal government point to budgetary surpluses before the end of the present decade, even under ambitious debt reduction scenarios.[15] Evidence of such structural imbalance has been used in the past to justify reviewing the division of tax room between the federal and provincial governments.

table 1

Federal and Provincial Revenues and Expenditures, Selected Calendar Years, 1950 to 1991
(in millions of dollars)

	Revenues			Expenditures		
	Federal	Provincial Excluding Grants	Ratio Federal/ Provincial	Federal Excluding Grants	Provincial Including Grants	Ratio Federal/ Provincial
1950	3 020	965	3.13	2 119	1 230	1.72
1955	5 008	1 377	3.64	4 356	1 814	2.40
1960	6 517	2 340	2.79	5 752	3 532	1.63
1965	9 097	4 945	1.84	7 149	6 324	1.13
1970	15 538	10 543	1.47	11 894	14 146	0.84
1975	31 817	22 292	1.43	27 970	31 569	0.89
1980	50 653	46 613	1.09	48 485	59 806	0.81
1981	65 005	54 565	1.19	58 233	69 596	0.84
1982	66 119	60 447	1.09	70 556	81 765	0.86
1983	69 634	66 511	1.05	76 990	90 070	0.85
1984	76 503	73 083	1.05	86 622	94 382	0.92
1985	83 237	77 292	1.08	92 915	102 635	0.91
1986	91 648	81 092	1.13	94 176	109 714	0.86
1987	100 771	89 774	1.12	98 788	115 284	0.86
1988	110 411	100 245	1.10	105 263	124 313	0.85
1989	117 989	107 102	1.10	114 093	133 050	0.86
1990	126 313	114 541	1.10	125 081	142 102	0.88
1991	132 929	115 145	1.15	135 443	154 257	0.88

Source: Canadian Tax Foundation, *The National Finances* (Toronto: Canadian Tax Foundation, 1992), Tables 3:11 and 3:13.

Accountability and Redistribution in a Federal System

The issue of fiscal responsibility in the presence of intergovernmental transfers is often discussed in terms of accountability and transparency. Generally speaking, making the level of government that provides the service responsible for taxing those who benefit is seen as favouring a greater degree of accountability. The principle of transparency, for its part, holds that it should be clear to taxpayers which level of government is responsible for funding and administering the programs and services delivered. In this way, taxpayers know which level of government to hold responsible for changes in service levels. Similarly, governments wishing to receive the political credit for programs financed through the taxes they levy tend to prefer a greater degree of visibility.

In Canada, transparency has been a significant problem in the areas of health care and post-secondary education. Many taxpayers are unclear as to the federal role in these programs. Some observers have even argued that this lack of federal visibility has made EPF a natural target for federal cutbacks.[16] Moreover, the lack of transparency means that the provinces end up shouldering much of the blame for reductions in services that may be attributable to federal cutbacks in transfer payments.

The relative importance of federal transfer payments to the provinces is perceived by many as causing problems of accountability for both levels of government. From the taxpayers' point of view, this issue is likely to take on added importance as governments take steps to deal with their respective debt/deficit problems. The principle of accountability must, however, be weighed against the competing principles of fiscal equity and fiscal efficiency in the presence of horizontal imbalance.[17]

Overall, the system of fiscal transfers results in a significant redistribution of centrally collected revenues, in favour, especially, of those provinces that are recipients under the fiscal equalization program. A similar pattern of net redistribution would occur, however, if all revenue and expenditure functions were fully centralized. For example, equal per-capita expenditures undertaken by a central government financed through uniform taxes would lead to a redistribution in favour of those regions with below-average fiscal capacities. Thus, while the extent of redistribution under a fully centralized system may be somewhat greater or less than under a decentralized system with intergovernmental transfers, in practice it is unlikely to differ significantly. The relevance of decentralized tax and expenditure authority in a federal system is that government policies can be tailored to suit differences in preferences and needs across provinces. The "disadvantages" associated with the reduction in accountability in the presence of intergovernmental transfers must be weighed against the "advantages" associated with centralized taxation and decentralized decision making. The point is that fiscal transfers permit, in principle, the attainment of the same standard of fiscal equity in a decentralized federation as would exist under a fully centralized system. Fiscal equity, in turn, guarantees greater fiscal efficiency — that is, there is no incentive for inefficient migration flows based on fiscal criteria. In this light, intergovernmental transfers are seen to be integral to the efficient functioning of both the economic and the social union.

From Principles to Institutions: The Fiscal Equalization Program

Equalization payments are recognized as the federal government's principal instrument in fulfilling its mandate to ensure a measure of equity in the services available across the country. The objective of the fiscal equalization program is to enable recipient provinces to provide "reasonably comparable" levels of public services at "reasonably comparable" levels of taxation. Under this program, the federal government provides unconditional cash transfers to the governments of those provinces whose overall fiscal capacity — measured as a province's capacity to raise revenues under the so-called Representative Tax System (RTS) — is below the equalization standard.

The RTS comprises a standardized set of 32 provincial revenue sources, including, among others, personal income tax, corporation income tax, sales tax and natural resource royalties. For each of these taxes, a province's revenue-generating capacity is calculated as the product of a standardized tax rate (the national average rate) and the per-capita value of the tax base. Each province's equalization entitlement per revenue source is then calculated as the difference between its revenue-generating potential and the corresponding equalization standard, multiplied by population. Those provinces with positive net overall entitlements — calculated across revenues sources — receive an equalization payment from the federal government.

For each revenue source, the equalization standard currently in use is the per-capita revenue-generating potential in the so-called representative five provinces — Quebec, Ontario, Manitoba, Saskatchewan and British Columbia. This particular standard was adopted in 1982 in order to diminish the influence of oil and gas royalties in Alberta in determining overall entitlements. The five-province standard is currently somewhat below the national average fiscal capacity.

Equalization operates as a gross scheme — that is, provinces with above-average fiscal capacities (based on the five-province standard) are not equalized down; rather, payments are made out of general federal revenues. The effect is to raise the fiscal capacity (the revenue-generating potential under the RTS) in the recipient provinces to the level of the five-province standard. In practice, equalization payments raise revenues in recipient provinces to a level that is approximately 92 percent of the corresponding national average. Actual per-capita revenues raised by provinces may well differ from the fiscal capacity indicators used to determine equalization entitlements. This is because of differences between actual provincial tax rates and/or tax bases and those used for the RTS.

Figure 3 and table 2 illustrate the effect of equalization payments on provinces' fiscal capacities. It is evident that the program has a significant impact in evening out provincial revenue-generating potentials. The recipients are the four Atlantic provinces (Newfoundland, Prince Edward Island, Nova Scotia and New Brunswick), Quebec, and two Prairie provinces (Manitoba and Saskatchewan). These are the so-called "have-not" provinces.

Table 2 presents indices of fiscal capacity by province for 1990-91. The first row represents relative fiscal capacities in the absence of equalization. These vary from a low of 62.4 percent of the national average in Newfoundland to 133 percent of the national average in Alberta. The effect of equalization is to reduce these fiscal disparities. After equalization, relative fiscal capacities range from 92.5 percent of the national average in the recipient provinces to an average of 105.4 percent in the remaining provinces. Even among these have provinces, however, there are significant differences, with Ontario's relative fiscal capacity at 103.2 percent of the national average, British Columbia's at 97.9 percent and Alberta's at 123.8 percent.

figure 3

Provincial Revenue-Generating Potential
Per Capita After Equalization
1992-93

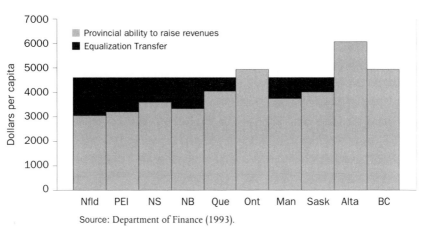

Source: Department of Finance (1993).

Growth in total annual equalization payments is, however, subject to a ceiling. The ceiling corresponds to the rate of growth in GDP over a given base year, applied to the value of equalization payments made in the base year. In the event that equalization entitlements exceed that ceiling, payments to the recipient provinces are scaled back accordingly, on an equal per-capita basis. This has the effect of reducing recipient provinces' relative fiscal capacities somewhat. As shown in Table 2, the index of fiscal capacity in 1990-91 for any recipient province was 91.2 percent of the national average once the growth ceiling is taken into account.

The growth ceiling was introduced in 1982. However, it did not affect entitlements until 1988-89 (the designated base year at that time was 1987-88). The ceiling had an impact in each subsequent fiscal year until 1992-93, at which point the program was renewed for a two-year period and the designated base year updated. Although the growth ceiling was expected to be an issue again in 1993-94,[18] this now appears less likely, given declining provincial tax revenues.

table 2

Indices of Provincial Fiscal Capacity,[1] 1990-91
(Canada = 100)

	Nfld	PEI	NS	NB	Que	Ont	Man	Sask	Alta	BC	Provinces		
											Receiving	Non-receiving[2]	Differential[3] in %
Before equalization	62.4	63.8	75.0	70.4	85.6	110.9	79.3	85.8	133.0	105.2	81.7	113.3	38.7
After equalization (pre-ceiling)	92.5	92.5	92.5	92.5	92.5	103.2	92.5	92.5	123.8	97.9	92.5	105.4	13.9
After equalization (post-ceiling)	91.2	91.2	91.2	91.2	91.2	104.2	91.2	91.2	125.0	98.8	91.2	106.4	16.7

[1] Includes local government revenues.
[2] Non-receiving provinces: Ontario, Alberta and British Columbia.
[3] As a percentage of the fiscal capacity of receiving provinces.

Source: Department of Finance, 5th estimate of equalization entitlements, 1990-1991.

One of the reasons equalization entitlements continue to run up against the growth ceiling is the impact of federal expenditure controls in other program areas such as EPF and CAP. To the extent that these have necessitated provincial tax increases to compensate for limits placed on growth in fiscal transfers, the resulting higher national average tax rates used in the equalization formula have increased equalization entitlements at a time when GDP growth is relatively low. An important implication of this is that, with the ceiling in effect, the have-not provinces are placed at a significant fiscal disadvantage in terms of compensating for the freeze in EPF entitlements. The same argument can be made concerning any additional provincial revenues that may be raised to cope, for instance, with increased welfare burdens resulting from the latest recession and cutbacks in other federal income security programs. These issues are addressed in more detail in the following chapters.

The fiscal equalization program is clearly directed at the federal government's mandate to make equalization payments contained in section 36 of the Constitution Act, 1982. However, it can also be argued that federal transfers under EPF and CAP complement the functioning of the fiscal equalization program.[19] As an equal per-capita transfer, EPF can be thought of as a provincial revenue source that is fully equalized. EPF is comprised of both a tax and cash transfer. The value of EPF tax points, of course, varies across provinces according to differences in fiscal capacities, even in the presence of equalization. However, this effect is neutralized through the allocation of the cash component of EPF, which is calculated on a residual basis. As a result, revenues are, in effect, redistributed from those provinces with above-average fiscal capacities to those with below-average fiscal capacities.

CAP transfers, on the other hand, can be viewed as a partial offset to asymmetric treatment of income transfers (through social assistance) and income taxes under the fiscal equalization program. For instance, if social assistance benefits were delivered entirely through some form of refundable tax credit, they would be buried within the provincial income tax system and reflected in provincial income tax revenues. However, under the current system, only provincial income taxes are eligible for fiscal equalization. CAP transfers partly compensate for this, at least to the extent that cost-matching transfers reflect differences in need for social assistance spending across provinces.

Figure 4 summarizes the impact of the three major transfer programs on provincial revenues per capita. The significance of equalization payments for provincial revenues in recipient provinces becomes evident. The other striking feature is the extent to which the three programs result in a substantial levelling of per-capita revenues.

figure 4

Provincial Revenues* Per Capita
After Major Fiscal Transfers
1992-93

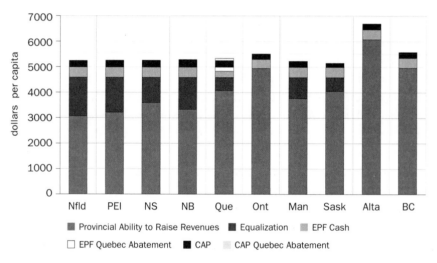

* Based on estimates of revenue-generating potential under the Representative Tax System.
Source: Department of Finance (1993).

three

epf and the devolution of tax room

One of the more significant changes to occur in the history of federal-provincial fiscal arrangements was the move to a system of block funding under EPF in 1977. From the point of view of the federal government, previous cost-sharing arrangements in the areas of health care and post-secondary education — both under provincial jurisdiction — had been an effective instrument through which to encourage the provinces to establish and develop programs in the "national interest." In the case of hospital insurance and medicare, the motivation was primarily to ensure the availability of essential health services for all Canadians on a similar basis and to coordinate the development of insured health services. Transfers for post-secondary education, for their part, were meant to provide sufficient financial resources to the provinces to meet rapidly growing requirements as the post-war generation came of age.[20]

As early as 1963, the federal government had announced its willingness to withdraw from programs that were considered "established" — that is, "programs that had been in effect long enough and that commanded sufficient public support to justify the presumption that they would not be discontinued by the provinces."[21] The federal government's intention was to provide additional tax room to the provinces as an alternative to specific-purpose grants. It was also intended that the provinces would then assume entire financial and administrative responsibility for these programs.

Some concrete proposals to that effect were put forward in the following years. A principal concern of the provinces, however, was that the fiscal compensation offered — through the transfer of tax room — would not produce sufficient revenues to replace the federal grants. By the mid-1970s, the federal government's efforts to institute alternative financing arrangements were stepped up, driven primarily by concerns about the lack of control over provincial program costs, which were consuming an increasing share of the federal budget. Ultimately, these concerns led to the implementation of block funding under EPF, designed as an equal per-capita transfer to be escalated annually in line with growth in GDP. This new approach to financing broke any remaining link between provincial program expenditures and the level of federal contributions. Also, since EPF included a transfer of tax room to the provinces, it was a significant further step in a process whereby, over the post-war period, the federal government had gradually been relinquishing income tax room.

The Division of Tax Room: Shifting Sands

The division of income tax room between the federal and provincial governments has been a central issue in federal-provincial fiscal relations since the Second World War. Under the 1941 Wartime Tax Agreements, the provinces agreed to give up temporarily the right to levy personal and corporate income taxes in return for agreed-upon levels of compensation — the so-called "tax rentals" — from the federal government. As a consequence, income taxation became completely centralized.

Among other things, this centralization of income taxation permitted the federal government to pursue broad equalization goals implicitly through unconditional revenue transfers. As well, during the post-war period, the federal government began making specific-purpose transfers available to the provinces in aid of various social programs.

The 1957 Federal-Provincial Tax Sharing Arrangements Act restructured the system of tax rentals according to the principle of derivation, under which the federal government returned to the provinces a fixed percentage of personal income tax revenues and of corporate income tax revenues collected within their jurisdictions — the so-called "standard abatements." In addition, explicit equalization payments were made according to a "top-two-province" standard. Under this system, per-capita revenues from the personal and corporate income taxes and from succession duties were equalized up to the average per-capita yield in Ontario and British Columbia. Therefore, revenues were effectively abated to participating provinces on a fully equalized per-capita basis.

The 1962 Federal-Provincial Fiscal Arrangements Act replaced the system of tax rentals with the Tax Collection Agreements that underlie the present system. Under the 1962 arrangements, the federal government yielded specific amounts of personal and corporation income tax room to the provinces by lowering its rate schedules and allowing the provinces to increase their own rates to fill the gap as they wished. Significantly, this placed the remaining provinces on an equal footing with Quebec, which had introduced its own personal income tax in 1954, at which time it had been granted equivalent tax room in lieu of the federal abatement. Per-capita revenues from direct taxation were still to be equalized to a "top-two-province" standard.

Through the Tax Collection Agreements, the federal government collects personal income taxes on behalf of all provinces except Quebec. Participating provinces must: (a) accept the federal definition of the base; (b) accept the federal definition of the rate structure; and (c) restrict themselves to a single rate of tax (to be set provincially), calculated as a percentage of basic federal tax (the so-called tax-on-tax framework). In addition, all provinces except Alberta, Ontario and Quebec participate in a tax collection agreement for the corporate income tax. Here, participating provinces must again accept the federal definition of the base, but they are able to set their own rates of tax levied against taxable income. Thus, the Tax Collection Agreements have allowed the full harmonization of bases and rate structures among participating provinces, features that are considered desirable from an economic efficiency standpoint.

In 1967, the federal government began providing special tax abatements and, subsequently, transfers of tax room to the provinces in lieu of specific-purpose transfers.[22] Initially, a special abatement on both the personal and corporate income taxes was provided in lieu of post-secondary education transfers. Subsequently, the EPF agreement of 1977 (discussed more fully below) involved a further transfer of personal income tax points to the provinces in lieu of health care grants. By 1977, as a result of this gradual devolution of tax room, the provinces had command of a basic 30.5 personal income tax points, as well as an additional 13.5 personal income tax points under the EPF agreements, plus a basic nine corporate income tax points and one additional corporate income tax point in respect of EPF.

Meanwhile, the equalization system had been modified in 1967. The list of revenue sources eligible for equalization was expanded beyond direct taxes. At the same time, the equalization standard was changed from a "top-two-province" standard to a national average standard. This was a significant departure from previous arrangements in terms of its revenue implications for provinces with deficient income tax capacities. Specifically, transfers of income tax room would only be equalized up to the national average standard; and this meant that the value of any transfer of income tax room would be greater for those provinces with above-average income tax capacities. In other words, transfers of income tax room would thus no longer be "fully equalized" as they had been in the past.

Established Programs Financing

From 1952 to 1967, the federal government's contributions to post-secondary education consisted of equal per-capita grants provided directly to the universities. Since 1967, federal contributions in this area have been established within the context of federal-provincial fiscal arrangements, with payments made directly to provincial governments. Initially, federal assistance comprised a cash and tax transfer designed to cover 50 percent of universities' total operating expenditures in each province. In part, this recognized that the per-capita value of the transferred tax room, even when equalized, would be less for those provinces with below-average fiscal capacities. This approach also took into account the fact that per-capita costs varied across provinces and that these variations could not be provided for through a straight tax transfer. Alternatively, provinces could opt for a straight per-capita cash transfer equivalent to national average per-capita university expenditures. Given that their operating expenditures were significantly below average, the Atlantic provinces, for instance, opted for the latter alternative. From 1973 to 1976, a growth ceiling (15 percent) was placed on the overall annual transfer. Generally speaking, however, the fact that the federal government covered half of university operating expenditures, with the remainder financed through a combination of student fees and provincial government grants, meant that the federal share of costs automatically exceeded that of the provinces.

Under the hospital insurance program implemented in 1958, federal transfer payments for in-patient services were determined as a per-capita grant equal to 25 percent of a province's per-capita costs plus 25 percent of national average per-capita costs. When the national medical care program was introduced in 1968, federal government transfers for health insurance were calculated as 50 percent of national average per-capita costs. In both cases, the fact that transfers were tied to the national average per-capita costs meant that provinces with below-average expenditures received in excess of 50 percent cost sharing while those with above-average expenditures received less than 50 percent cost sharing. To the extent that per-capita expenditures reflected provincial fiscal capacities, this transfer formula included an implicit element of equalization. However, since half of the federal contribution for hospital insurance was tied to actual provincial per-capita costs, the level of transfers per capita still varied significantly across provinces.

The 1977 Federal-Provincial Fiscal Arrangements and Established Programs Financing Act was designed to consolidate the transfers under these three programs into a single block-funding arrangement. The initial EPF arrangement consisted of a further transfer of tax points plus an equal per-capita cash transfer equivalent to half of the federal transfers for health care and post-secondary education in 1975-76 (the base year). The number of EPF tax points — 13.5 personal and one corporate income — was designed to yield per-capita revenues in the two richest provinces (Ontario and BC) equivalent to half the average per-capita transfer in the base year. The tax points were equalized up to the national standard used at the time under the fiscal equalization formula. However, since the value of the tax transfer was intended to be equal to the cash transfer for all provinces, supplementary cash transfers — transitional payments — were also necessary to raise the per-capita yield (inclusive of fiscal equalization) from the transferred tax points to that in the "top two provinces." In subsequent years, the cash transfer was to be escalated in accordance with growth in per-capita GNP and population growth in each province, while the revenue yield from the tax points would increase along with personal and corporate tax revenues.

The move to equal per-capita cash transfers for established programs meant that provinces previously receiving per-capita contributions above the national average (due to higher than average program expenditures) would receive less under the new arrangements. In response to this, adjustments were made to level down, over a period of five years, the funds to those provinces that had received above-average per-capita transfers. In addition, Quebec's cash entitlement was to be adjusted downward to take into account the special abatement of 8.5 tax points remaining from earlier opt-out arrangements.

Notionally, 17.4 percent of the EPF transfer was designated for medicare, 50.5 percent for hospital insurance and 32.1 percent for post-secondary education. These percentages reflect the respective shares of federal transfers in the three program areas nationally in 1975-76. Of course, this did not necessarily reflect the actual distribution in individual provinces. For instance, while in Quebec over 35 percent of federal established programs contributions were in the form of post-secondary education transfers during the 1975-76 base year, the corresponding share was only 25 percent (well below the national average) in the Atlantic provinces.

It was inevitable that, with time, EPF would cease to be an equal per-capita transfer (cash plus tax), since the value of the tax transfer in provinces with relatively high fiscal capacities would eventually exceed the (equal per-capita) value of the cash transfer. In order to ensure that EPF entitlements remained on an equal per-capita basis, the program was modified in 1982. From this point, the growth escalator was to apply to the total per-capita value of EPF entitlements. The per-capita cash transfer in any province was then calculated as the difference between total entitlement per capita (equal for all provinces) and the per-capita value of the tax transfer (including any associated equalization payments). In Quebec's case, the value of the additional 8.5 tax point abatement was added to the value of the tax transfer. Figure 5 illustrates the various components involved in calculating the value of EPF entitlements by province.

figure 5

Provincial EPF Entitlements Per Capita by Component
1992-93

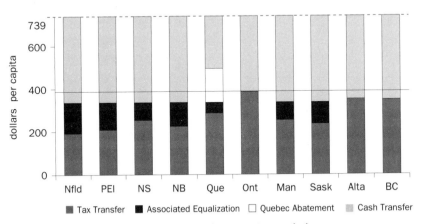

Note: The horizontal line represents the top province standard.
Source: Department of Finance (1993).

The provinces argue that the federal government has subsequently reneged on the terms of EPF. This is seen to be the case particularly as a result of the various modifications made by the federal government to the escalator used to calculate growth in EPF entitlements from year to year. Initially set as a three-year compound moving average of GNP growth per capita, the rate of growth of per-capita entitlements for the post-secondary education component was limited to six percent for 1983-84 and five percent for 1984-85 as part of the federal government's "6 & 5" program. From 1986-87 to 1989-90, the EPF escalator was reduced to the rate of growth of per-capita GDP less two percentage points. This was expected to be scaled down further to 3 percentage points below per-capita GDP growth for 1990-91. This move was preempted, however, by the two-year freeze on total per-capita entitlements announced in the 1990 federal budget. Following the 1991 budget, the freeze on EPF transfers was extended to the end of 1994-95, at which point an escalator equivalent to the growth in per-capita GDP less three percent will apply. Thus, a growth rate on per-capita entitlements of 14 percent in 1977-78 fell to 5.8 percent in 1986-87, to just under five percent in 1989-90 and has been held at zero since then.

According to estimates produced by the government of Ontario, the provinces' total revenue shortfall resulting from the modifications to the EPF escalator may be as high as $33.6 billion up to and including 1992-93. For Ontario alone, the cumulative loss since 1982-83 is estimated at $12.3 billion. The revenue shortfall for all provinces combined is projected to be $7.3 billion in 1992-93, with Ontario's share at $2.7 billion.[23] The government of Quebec estimates that its resulting revenue shortfall for 1992-93 will be just under $2 billion. Moreover, it argues that to maintain service levels (i.e., to compensate for the loss in transfers), the province will have to increase its tax burden by an additional $285 million relative to the have provinces, since the cutbacks were not adjusted on the basis of provincial fiscal capacities.[24]

Reductions in EPF cash transfers have posed particular problems for the recipient provinces under fiscal equalization in the presence of the overall limit on aggregate equalization payments. The equalization ceiling, which limits entitlements to the rate of growth of GDP over a base year, has two effects. First, when the ceiling is reached, equalization entitlements have to be scaled back accordingly, which means that the effective equalized value of the EPF tax transfer is reduced somewhat. Ironically, this effect results in an offsetting adjustment in the residual EPF cash transfer. Second, if the provinces increase taxes in response to reductions in EPF cash entitlements, the resulting increases in equalization entitlements are not payable if the ceiling is in effect. In other words, beyond the ceiling, additional provincial revenues must be raised entirely from own-revenue sources. Since own-source fiscal capacities vary markedly across provinces, this requires significantly greater rate increases in those provinces with below-average fiscal capacities if the revenue shortfall is to be made up.

The marginal impact of a $1 per-capita increase in own-source revenues in 1990-91 has been estimated to be, on average, 39 percent greater in the have-not provinces than in the have provinces; that is, the tax effort required to replace $1 per capita in reduced EPF cash transfers is 39 percent greater in the have-not than in the have provinces. The figures vary significantly by province. Relative to the average for the three have provinces, the index is 170 in Newfoundland, 168 in Prince Edward Island, 148 in Nova Scotia, 156 in New Brunswick, 134 in Quebec, 102 in

Ontario, 142 in Manitoba, 133 in Saskatchewan, 85 in Alberta and 108 in British Columbia. In any case, even if there had been no ceiling, it is estimated that the additional tax effort required in 1990-91 by the have-not provinces to compensate for each $1 per-capita cut in EPF would have been 17 percent greater than in the have provinces.[25]

The freeze on per-capita EPF entitlements has also resulted in a faster rate of erosion of the cash component than would have been the case otherwise. The cash component is calculated as the residual between total entitlement (frozen on a per-capita basis) and the value of the tax transfer. Given that the value of the tax transfer rises over time, this has a corresponding effect on the value of the cash transfer. Initial projections at the time the freeze was implemented indicated that federal cash transfers under EPF would fall to zero by the end of the decade unless an annual escalator was reinstated. Because of Quebec's special tax abatement, the value of the cash transfer in respect of post-secondary education to Quebec was projected to fall to zero by the middle of the decade and the remaining health care cash component soon after.

This scenario has raised questions as to the appropriate federal response should cash entitlements in fact become negative. Should these be recouped through reductions in other transfers or should a situation be allowed to emerge where the effective per-capita transfer differs from province to province? This is what would happen in Quebec if, for example, a corresponding adjustment were not made for the negative cash entitlements.

In addition, the erosion of the cash component of EPF has raised questions as to the federal government's continued ability to exercise leverage over the provinces with regard to the so-called "national standards" in health care. One of the motives for the shift to block funding for health care and post-secondary education had been to give the provinces greater autonomy and flexibility, by eliminating the link between provincial program spending and the level of federal transfers. However, this aspect of EPF soon gave rise to concerns over the potential erosion of prior program conditions related to health care. Under previous arrangements, cost-sharing provisions entailed a certain degree of federal monitoring that automatically encouraged compliance with the program conditions contained in the Hospital Insurance and Diagnostic Services Act of 1957 and the Medical Care Act of 1966.

The perception of a loss of federal leverage under EPF was addressed through the restatement of the basic principles of medicare in the Canada Health Act of 1984. The Act gives the federal government explicit authority to withhold EPF cash transfers (on a dollar-for-dollar basis) from provinces that allow extra-billing or user fees. This issue gained considerable attention in 1986, when the growing practice of extra-billing in a number of provinces triggered matching reductions in EPF cash entitlements. These amounts were withheld from the provinces until such time as they passed legislation banning extra billing. At present, the position of the federal government appears to be that, should EPF cash be insufficient to maintain leverage, reductions will then be made in transfers in other program areas.[26]

The recession appears to have given a new lease on life to the cash component of EPF, as the growth in value of the tax transfer has been much lower than initially anticipated. Nevertheless, the Canada Health Act will remain the subject of considerable debate between those who consider it to be the mechanism through which national health care "standards" are defined and implemented and those who interpret it primarily as a statement of principles and objectives. Some of the issues involved are discussed below.

Assessment of EPF

There is an interesting equalization dimension to the interplay between cash and tax transfers under EPF. Prior to 1967, the transfer of tax room to the provinces was equalized to the "top-two-province" standard then in effect and therefore produced equal per-capita yields across provinces — that is, transferred tax room was "fully equalized." However, the adoption in 1967 of a national average standard for fiscal equalization and in 1982 of the representative five-province standard rendered the matter of transferring income tax room to the provinces more complex. Thereafter, a variable cash component would be required in addition to the fiscal equalization associated with the tax transfer, in order to preserve the principle of equal per-capita yields.

The fact that EPF is calculated as an equal per-capita entitlement and that the cash component is determined to be the difference between the equal per-capita transfer and the value of the tax points after equalization therefore allows for an implicit form of supplementary equalization. This is illustrated in figure 5. Although equalization of the EPF tax points raises the per-capita yield in the have-not provinces to the representative five-province standard, the per-capita yield remains below that of Ontario. In part, then, the cash transfer raises the per-capita yield in all provinces[27] up to a "top province" standard — in this case, Ontario, as indicated by the horizontal line. Above that level, the cash component works as an equal per-capita transfer. In other words, the difference between the per-capita cash transfer in Ontario and that in other provinces constitutes a form of supplementary equalization.

It is worth spelling out some further implications of the equal per-capita nature of the transfer. Since the value of the transferred tax points is eligible for equalization, all have-not provinces receive the same per-capita cash transfer. As figure 5 shows, the per-capita cash transfer is correspondingly lower for those have provinces whose tax transfer has a value greater than the equalization standard. It is interesting to note, however, that a province such as Alberta, which is not a recipient of fiscal equalization but may, in some years, be fiscally deficient in the income tax categories, might end up receiving the greatest per-capita EPF cash transfer among all provinces. For example, this was the case during the 1990-91 fiscal year. Full equalization of this sort could not be accomplished through a simple transfer of tax room to the provinces.[28]

This argument can be taken one step further. In a sense, EPF is equivalent to a fully equalized transfer of tax room to the provinces, where the effective number of transferred tax points corresponds to the total EPF transfer (cash plus tax) as a percentage of federal income tax revenues.[29] Looked at in this way, it can be argued that, unlike previous transfers of tax room, the effective number of tax points "transferred" under EPF (that is, the actual number of tax points transferred, plus the notional number of additional tax points represented by the cash payment) has fallen over time. The reasons for this are straightforward. The rate of growth of per-capita EPF entitlements was tied to the rate of growth in per-capita GDP starting in 1982. However, because of progressive tax rates, per-capita personal income tax revenues have grown faster than the rate of growth of per-capita GDP. As a result, the effective number of tax points "transferred" under EPF is lower today than when the program was introduced. Moreover, the subsequent adjustments to the GDP escalator made by the federal government as part of its expenditure control programs over the past decade have accelerated this reduction. Viewed in this light, it might be argued that the federal government has been unilaterally pre-empting the "tax room" earmarked for provincial financing of established programs in order to pursue other objectives.[30]

Unfinished Business

The main thrust of the discussion in the previous section is that the devolution of income tax room to the provinces with respect to the established programs remains as unfinished business on the federal-provincial fiscal relations agenda. Program design and federal fiscal restraint have gradually reduced the number of income tax points effectively transferred in 1977. This is entirely inconsistent with previous transfers of tax room. In order to achieve complete fiscal disentanglement, tax room should be devolved to the provinces once and for all with respect to the established programs.

One way of achieving this within the existing EPF framework would be for the federal government to cede the value of the cash component of EPF to the provinces as an explicit tax abatement rather than actually transfer further tax room. That is, a fixed percentage of federal income tax revenues would be earmarked for the established programs. These revenues would not, however, be distributed according to collections by province; rather, they would be pooled for purposes of "topping up" the per-capita value of the existing EPF tax transfer by province to its fully equalized value — basically the sort of supplementary equalization which we discussed earlier — with any surplus being distributed on an equal per-capita basis. The federal role in funding social programs, then, would simply be to coordinate revenue pooling through centralized collection and redistribution.[31]

The number of tax points to be abated under EPF would need to be negotiated. It could be set at the effective number of tax points associated with EPF had the original block-funding amounts been escalated in accordance with GDP to the present time, less the total equalized value of the EPF tax transfer. Alternatively, it could be the number of tax points associated with the current level of total cash transfers under EPF. No doubt, other reference points might be explored.[32] What is important is that, once set, there would be no further erosion of the effective number of tax points transferred under EPF. Equally, however, their value would rise and fall in step with income tax revenues.

Whither National Standards?

In comparing the various options available to the federal government in the context of fiscal arrangements, some observers have described block funding as a poor compromise between a shared-cost approach (with all that this implies in terms of conditionality and federal monitoring) and a "clean" transfer of tax room (implying a complete withdrawal of federal intervention).[33] In a sense, the federal government's objective in shifting to block funding under EPF was to do a little bit of both. On the one hand, it wanted to eliminate the spending incentives associated with cost sharing and add a greater degree of control over the growth of its own expenditures. This was accomplished by shifting part of the fiscal responsibility to the provinces via the tax transfer and by severing the link between federal transfers and provincial program spending, thus allowing provinces more autonomy and flexibility. On the other hand, EPF arrangements were meant to ensure a continuing federal participation in these program areas; this was to be achieved through a transfer program that was semi-conditional, via the cash component and the Canada Health Act, and "semi-earmarked." Transfers for health care and post-secondary education were issued using an allocation formula that reflected the federal national contributions in 1975-76, under the implicit assumption that the funds were not meant for other purposes, even though such earmarking is not binding on the provinces. Given these initial objectives, it might be argued that EPF has been only "semi" successful. Other critics have been harsher in their assessment. For instance, based on an assessment of the nature of the "national," and, therefore, federal interest in health care and post-secondary education and the actual impact of federal involvement through block funding, Maslove argues that EPF is in effect a "failed program."[34]

The dichotomy between federal and provincial perspectives concerning the tax transfer under EPF is a central issue. For the federal government, the tax transfer has been considered as nothing more than an instrument to transfer federal fiscal resources to the provinces to help them with their expenditure responsibilities in these designated program areas. From the provinces' point of view, however, EPF involved a devolution of tax room similar to other adjustments in the division of tax room that had occurred in the past. Revenue yields associated with EPF have simply been lumped in with general revenues and allocated accordingly. Consequently, one of the objectives of the federal government, to direct funds to designated program areas, is not fulfilled by block funding.[35]

Another issue that raises even more controversy concerns the federal government's role in enforcing "national standards" in program areas. Since, in practice, there have never been any federal conditions or standards for post-secondary education, the issues here pertain only to health care and, in particular, the five broad principles enunciated under the 1984 Canada Health Act — public administration, comprehensiveness, universality, portability and accessibility. As mentioned previously, one of the key concerns about the decline in the value of the cash transfers under EPF has been that the federal government would lose its ability to enforce the principles of the Canada Health Act.

Health care has become a prominent policy issue in recent years, in part because of an increased awareness of the relative importance and the rate of growth of health care costs and also because, as the pressures for reform continue to mount, Canadians have strongly asserted their support for the system in place and its underlying principles.[36] The degree of concern was clearly demonstrated during the last round of constitutional negotiations, when federal involvement in social programs was seen to be at issue. The debate centred on whether the basic principle of universality might be at risk. At the same time, there is now greater awareness that a national health care system does not necessarily imply complete uniformity in health services provided across provinces. The range of services insured and the fee schedules can differ considerably from province to province while conforming to the broad principles of the national system. In particular, portability and universal coverage do not appear to be at issue.[37]

However, whether or not the costs of the present system can be met remains a major concern. In this light, the extent to which the Canada Health Act constrains provinces in their search for new instruments to control health care costs needs to be addressed. The evidence is not clear in this regard. Some observers have argued that the Canada Health Act reinforces approaches to service delivery that are out of date. In particular, the legislation is seen to contain built-in incentives for more doctors and more institutions at a time when policy requirements appear to be in the direction of a more preventive and more efficient system.[38] There are others who argue, however, that there really are no national standards in health care and that, other than the specific provisions concerning user fees and extra billing, the provinces have had considerable discretion in developing distinct health care policies and programs. According to Tuohy, it is in fact surprising that the differences are not even greater "...given the loose constraints of the federal legislation."[39]

Whatever the case may be, it is clear that as provinces continue to deal with the issue of health care costs, the difficult decisions ahead will call for greater emphasis on accountability and transparency concerning both the financing and administration of the system. Also, one of the recognized advantages of decentralization is the ability of lower levels of government to acknowledge the geographical diversity in demand and need for public services and to experiment with new modes of production and delivery. These considerations lend further support to the disentanglement option proposed in this chapter. Finally, the process of health care reform is already under way and provinces have shown an interest in comparing approaches and consulting with each other on these issues. Therefore, it does not seem farfetched to suggest that the provinces would be both willing and in a better position than the federal government to establish a set of acceptable standards, or a code of conduct, with regard to a national health care system. National standards do not necessarily have to be federal standards.[40]

four

the federal-provincial dimension
to income security

The Canada Assistance Plan (CAP) is the only remaining major federal-provincial cost-sharing program and the instrument through which the federal government provides transfers to the provinces for social assistance and social services programs. As such, it is an integral part of Canada's income security network. The current pressures to review and reform CAP are twofold. First, the practice of open-ended cost matching is increasingly difficult to maintain in an environment of expenditure control and cost-cutting measures directed at the debt/deficit problem. It could even be argued that the five percent annual growth ceiling imposed on CAP transfers to the have provinces since 1990 (the so-called "cap on CAP") has already, *de facto,* put an end to this type of arrangement. Second, social assistance, which was initially designed as the program of "last resort," has increasingly become the safety net for scores of unemployed employables. As governments make the transition from passive to active support measures to deal with this problem and the resulting costs, the need for reform becomes more apparent. Various studies and commission reports[41] have for some time now emphasized the need for a better integration of the entire income security network in Canada and the importance of measures implemented through the tax system in providing income supplements and work incentives. It is also now recognized that there is a need for greater flexibility and innovation at the provincial level in defining "active" income support strategies that are effective.

These pressures will inevitably lead to a review of CAP, but this need not spell the demise of cost sharing as such. Unlike programs in health care and post-secondary education, we do not see a move to block funding as being warranted. The argument concerning these programs was that they were well "established" and would be maintained by the provinces even with reduced federal involvement. As the debate on income security reform continues, propelled by fiscal and economic considerations, it is clear that the label "established" does not apply to social assistance and social services programs. More importantly, any alternative to CAP will have to take into account the constitutional responsibilities of each level of government in the area of income redistribution, the role of social assistance as part of the system of income security as well as the counter-cyclical nature of the programs concerned.

The Tangled Safety Net[42]

The Federal Role in Income Security Programs

As a matter of "a local or private nature," responsibility for the delivery of social policy rests with the provinces under the Constitution Act, 1867. Similarly, the Act assigned responsibility in matters of "property and civil rights" to the provinces under which responsibility for unemployment insurance was deemed to be included. The Rowell-Sirois Commission held that the federal government should have responsibility for the relief of unemployed employables, whereas the provinces should maintain responsibility for assistance to unemployables. In addition, the Commission argued that the provinces should "be enabled financially to perform these services adequately."[43] The federal government was assigned formal responsibility for unemployment insurance in 1940, following a constitutional amendment.

The Constitution Act, 1982 provided explicit grounds for federal spending in the social policy field. First, the Charter of Rights and Freedoms enshrined mobility and equality rights of persons. Second, and perhaps more importantly, section 36 committed both levels of government to "promoting equal opportunities for the well-being of Canadians" and "providing essential public services of reasonable quality to all Canadians." This conferred a broad equity mandate on the federal government, one that, in the absence of legislative authority in the social policy field, could be fulfilled primarily through the use of the federal spending power. Over time, federal responsibility for stabilization policy and income redistribution, the implementation of programs of national interest and the issue of spillover effects between provinces have justified the extent of federal involvement. The federal government has been involved directly through its own programs and indirectly through cost-sharing arrangements to help finance provincial initiatives.

As a result, the system of income security in Canada has evolved into a complex mix of programs and measures involving the three levels of government.[44] Of course, the level of complexity is also a reflection of the heterogeneity of the needs to be addressed (e.g., those of the elderly, the disabled, single-parent families, the working poor and the unemployed) and the variety of measures and instruments that are used to address these needs (e.g., cash transfers, subsidies, in-kind provisions and personal income tax measures).[45]

Table 3 lists the main income security programs and related expenditures for 1990-91. Federal income support for the elderly and the unemployed represent the majority of expenditures, accounting for close to 88 percent of federal spending on income security. Under the Canada Assistance Plan, the federal government also makes transfer payments to provinces to cover a portion of the costs of provincial welfare programs. Federal payments for social assistance benefits represented approximately eight percent of total federal income security expenditures in 1990-91.

Income Redistribution via the Tax System

The federal government also pursues income redistribution objectives implicitly through the personal income tax system. Tax expenditures occur as a result of tax deductions, tax credits and refundable tax credits. Various reforms implemented since 1987 have improved the efficiency of tax measures in targeting relief to the needy. Personal exemptions and selected deductions have been converted to credits, increasing the value of these for low-income tax-filers. In addition, the extended use of refundable tax credits (child tax credit and sales tax credit) enables the

table 3

Income Security Programs in Canada
Benefit Expenditures by Program,
1990-91

Program	$ million	% of Total
Federal Programs		
Old Age Security, Guaranteed Income Supplement,		
and Spouse's Allowance (total)	17,130	25%
Canada Pension Plan	10,541	16%
Veterans' Programs	1,200	2%
Family Allowances	2,736	4%
Child Tax Credit	2,109	3%
Unemployment Insurance	14,468	21%
Sub-Total	48,184	71%
Cost-shared Programs		
Social Assistance (a)		
Federal	4,440	7%
Provincial	4,559	7%
Sub-Total	8,999	14%
Provincial Programs		
Provincial Tax Grants and		
Income Supplements (b)	2,734	4%
Worker's Compensation	4,315	6%
Quebec Pension Plan	3,224	5%
Sub-Total	10,273	15%
Total	67,456	100%

Note: (a): Social Assistance total from Health and Welfare. Estimates of federal share from
Canada Assistance Plan Annual Report.

(b): Figure for 1989-90; 1990-91 not available.

Source: Health and Welfare Canada, 1993.

payment of income-tested transfers to low-income individuals, including those without tax liabilities. The value of these tax expenditures in terms of forgone tax revenues is far from negligible. For 1989, the estimated cost to the federal government of selected personal income tax expenditures related to social policy objectives was on the order of $34.4 billion.[46] That compares with $46.9 billion in direct federal expenditures on income security programs for the same year.

Although personal income taxation is a shared tax field under the Constitution Act, the terms of the Tax Collection Agreements give the federal government substantial control over the way in which income redistribution in particular, and equity goals in general, may be pursued through the personal income tax code. While this system has resulted in significant harmonization in the personal income tax field, one of its disadvantages has been to restrict the provinces in their ability to implement and integrate their own income security measures through the personal income tax system. Provinces have been allowed to introduce low-income tax reductions as well as income-tested credits, but only to a limited extent and subject to the approval of the federal government.[47] Also, because of the terms of the Tax Collection Agreements, it can be argued that all the provinces except Quebec are implicitly sharing the cost of federal tax expenditures.[48]

The fact that Quebec administers its own personal income tax system has enabled that province to achieve a considerable degree of integration of its income support programs as well as to pursue distinct social policy objectives within a structure of rates, base and tax credits that essentially parallels the federal model. Quebec has followed the lead of the federal government in converting personal exemptions to credits but provides relatively more generous child tax credits in combination with family allowance supplements and lump-sum payments for new-born children as part of a pro-family policy. Since 1988, the province has also offered a comprehensive parental wage assistance program, known as APPORT,[49] aimed at encouraging the working poor to remain in the workforce and UI and welfare recipients to join the workforce. The program is based on three elements: a wage supplement, reimbursement of 55 percent of daycare expenses, and a housing allowance. In addition, families eligible for assistance under the program do not pay provincial income tax. The program is not presently eligible for cost sharing under CAP; this, however, is currently under review.

There is some indication that the provinces are increasingly finding the current Tax Collection Agreements to be insufficiently flexible in permitting them to address their own social and economic priorities through the income tax code.[50] The federal and provincial governments have been exploring alternative models, designed to give the provinces greater flexibility in tax policy and to promote transparency while at the same time maintaining the desirable features of a harmonized system. Proposals for modification of the Tax Collection Agreements are contained in a recent federal government report on personal income tax coordination.[51] A common aspect of these alternative models is that provincial tax would be levied against taxable income instead of as a fixed percentage of basic federal tax, as is currently the case. This would obviate the need for the various tax credits and "add-on" tax measures introduced by the provinces over time to effect their own redistributive and/or economic development goals within the constraints of the tax-on-tax system. Rather, there would be the same common set of non-refundable credits and associated eligibility criteria as at present, but provinces would be able to set values for these and establish their own income thresholds and reduction rates.

One important question here is the extent to which a system of provincial rates applied to taxable income based on standardized credits would enable the sort of experimentation in integrating social assistance and personal income taxes that has occurred in Quebec. What seems clear, however, is that any review of the Tax Collection Agreements will have to take into account the need for better integration of the income security system and allow the provinces a greater degree of flexibility within a common framework.

The Canada Assistance Plan

Objectives and Outcomes

The federal government has maintained a significant presence in the financing of provincial programs in social assistance and social services through its participation in the Canada Assistance Plan. CAP has been in place since 1966 and is now the only remaining major federal-provincial cost-sharing program. In 1992-93, total cash transfers under this program amounted to just under $6.5 billion. This is a significant amount even when compared with cash transfers under the other two major transfer programs — fiscal equalization at just over $8.4 billion and EPF at just over $9.3 billion.

The main purpose of the Canada Assistance Act of 1966 was to consolidate and expand the provisions of prior categorical cost-shared programs: unemployment assistance, old age assistance, blind persons allowances and disabled persons allowances. Although the federal government was to share in eligible costs incurred by the provinces under the Plan, the provinces remained solely responsible for the administration of the programs including their design, comprehensiveness, eligibility requirements and method of delivery.

From its inception, the stated objectives of CAP have been the provision of adequate assistance to persons in need and the prevention and removal of the causes of poverty and dependence on public assistance. In addition to a needs-test requirement, only minimal conditions were imposed on provinces: specifically, that no residency restrictions be applied; that relevant statistical and financial information be provided; and that an appeal process in respect of social assistance be put in place.

The objectives were to be achieved, in part, by sharing on a 50-50 basis in the cost of programs with the provinces. The Act also stipulates that assistance is to be available on the basis of need rather than means. The intent was to eliminate differences in levels of assistance and eligibility according to particular characteristics of potential beneficiaries (e.g., the blind, the elderly). In addition, CAP provisions introducing cost-sharing arrangements for welfare services were intended to address the issues of poverty and dependency prevention by providing financial incentives for provinces to develop and expand social services in the context of a national anti-poverty program.

At the time it was introduced, the general needs test was seen to be an innovative policy instrument. The test involves assessing the relation between resources (assets and other financial resources) and budgetary requirements. However, in practice, the needs test has been used only as a very general guideline to establish eligibility. Individual provinces have had almost total discretion both in defining the precise conditions of eligibility and in setting levels of assistance. In most cases, the need assessment is not reflected in the levels of benefits granted as these are generally predetermined on a scale basis. Although CAP was meant to eliminate the categorical approach to providing assistance, all provinces assign different levels of assistance according to particular characteristics (e.g., for the disabled, single parents, the unemployable and the employable).[52]

Since the mid-70s, the federal government has also issued guidelines setting limits on cost-sharing levels under CAP. For instance, there are guidelines as to the maximum amount of employment income and allowances for work-related expenses and liquid assets that can be exempt. However, the rules of individual provinces vary significantly within these guidelines.[53]

As a result, welfare programs differ significantly across provinces both in terms of coverage and levels of assistance. Per-capita expenditures on programs eligible under CAP mask a marked variation across provinces in

table 4

Transfers to the Provinces Under the Canada Assistance Plan,
1989-90

Province	Total ($ million)	$/Capita	Index of need[1]	Index of generosity[2]
Newfoundland	101.0	177.0	104	84
Prince Edward Island	23.9	183.7	86	105
Nova Scotia	157.2	177.4	118	75
New Brunswick	158.9	221.2	130	84
Quebec[3]	1,681.1	251.2	121	103
Ontario	1,906.2	199.0	86	115
Manitoba	194.5	179.3	86	103
Saskatchewan	152.9	151.7	78	96
Alberta	517.0	213.4	84	126
British Columbia	720.0	235.8	107	109

[1] Welfare recipients per capita relative to the national average expressed as an index of 100.
[2] Expenditures per recipients relative to the national average expressed as an index of 100.
[3] Inclusive of $574.7 million value of the special abatement to Quebec.

Source: Robin W. Boadway and Paul A.R. Hobson, *Intergovernmental Fiscal Relations in Canada,* (Toronto: Canadian Tax Foundation, 1993).

terms of benefit levels paid to recipients as well as numbers of recipients as a percentage of population. This is illustrated by the need and generosity indices presented in table 4. Those provinces with relatively large numbers of recipients as a percentage of their population tend to provide relatively low benefit levels. Benefits levels appear to be loosely correlated with provincial fiscal capacities.

Approximately 80 percent of CAP expenditures fall under its assistance provisions. This category includes assistance benefits as well as spending in homes for special care (e.g., homes for the elderly and the disabled, child-care facilities, homes for battered women and children), certain health care costs and the majority of child welfare expenditures. Cash welfare payments are the main item, with the federal contribution amounting to $4.5 billion in 1991-92 (63 percent of total payments). Most of the remaining 20 percent of CAP expenditures are for welfare services (e.g., casework, counselling, home support services, rehabilitation etc.), including administrative costs. CAP transfers for work activity projects accounted for only half of one percent of total payments in 1990-91 ($3.7 million).

Over the past twenty years, federal CAP payments to the provinces have almost tripled in real terms. As figure 7 demonstrates, this increase is largely related to the growth in the numbers of assistance recipients. With each recession, the welfare caseload has increased dramatically, while the number of beneficiaries has tended to remain stable at the higher level through subsequent recoveries. Between 1988 and 1991, the number of persons assisted under CAP rose to 2.7 million from 1.8 million, an increase of 47 percent. This sharp increase is, in large part, explained by events in Ontario, where a combination of changes in eligibility requirements and the toll of the latest recession have led to a doubling of the caseload in the last few years.

The link between economic cycles and the trend in the number of people on welfare has an additional dimension — one commonly referred to as the "UI/CAP interface." For instance, the significant drop experienced in the number of social assistance beneficiaries between 1971 and 1974 resulted not only from the decline in the unemployment rate but also from the changes in the Unemployment Insurance Act in 1971, which relaxed UI eligibility rules. It is also believed that the same factors, this time operating in the opposite direction, were at play between 1981 and 1984,

figure 6

Allocation of Expenditures Under the Canada Assistance Plan
by Program Component, 1991-92

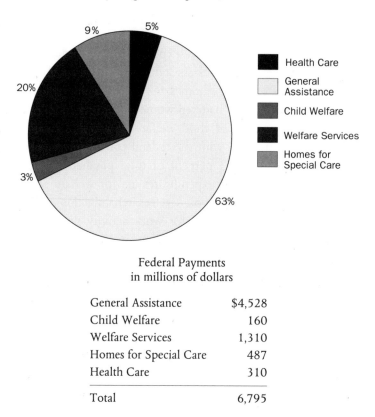

Federal Payments
in millions of dollars

General Assistance	$4,528
Child Welfare	160
Welfare Services	1,310
Homes for Special Care	487
Health Care	310
Total	6,795

Source: Canada Assistance Plan Annual Report, 1991-92

when UI eligibility rules were tightened. In effect, the interaction between programs works both ways. For instance, provincial make-work projects have been shown to reduce welfare caseloads as people become eligible for UI benefits after having worked the required number of weeks.[54]

This interaction between welfare and UI can be argued to be consistent with the intent of CAP, which is to share in the costs of provision of income support to needy individuals who have exhausted all other avenues available to them (including all other income support programs designed to

figure 7

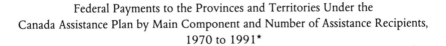

Federal Payments to the Provinces and Territories Under the
Canada Assistance Plan by Main Component and Number of Assistance Recipients,
1970 to 1991*

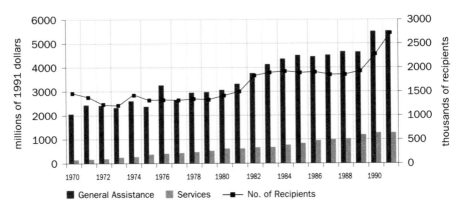

* Data for payments in 1991 are estimates.

Source: Health and Welfare Canada, *Canada Assistance Plan Annual Report, 1991-1992*
(Ottawa: Minister of Supply and Services, 1993).

address the specific needs of the unemployed, the elderly, the disabled, veterans, etc.). This is why social assistance is often referred to as the program of last resort. Consequently, the number of individuals on social assistance and the costs involved can be expected to fluctuate according to changes in eligibility and benefit levels made under other programs, many of which are federal. However, it can also be argued that, being structured in this way, the programs of last resort are limited in their ability to address specific problems and are subject to overflow when the system fails elsewhere.

Figure 8 displays the variations in regional patterns in terms of the number of assistance recipients as a percentage of population. The graph shows the consistently high ratios of dependency in the less wealthy provinces as well as the impact of economic cycles and migration patterns on particular provinces at particular points in time. The cases of British Columbia (1980-86) and Ontario (1988-92) are particularly striking. These patterns illustrate both the differing regional effects of economic cycles and the difficulties involved in predicting the need for and cost of social assistance.

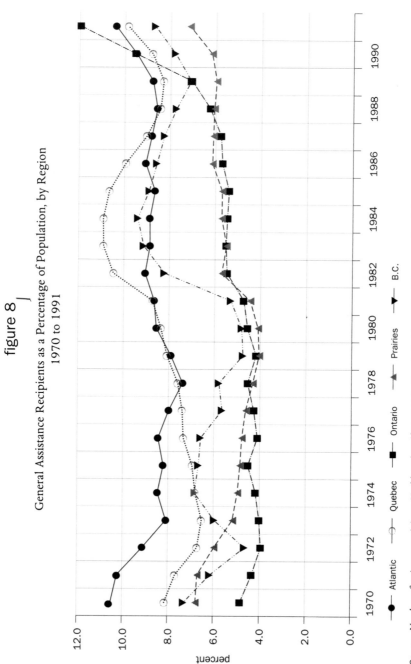

figure 8

General Assistance Recipients as a Percentage of Population, by Region
1970 to 1991

Source: Number of assistance recipients: Health and Welfare Canada, Canada Assistance Plan Directorate. Population: Statistics Canada, cat. 11-210. IRPP estimates.

Current Issues and Constraints

The major change concerning CAP programs in the past twenty years is undoubtedly the dramatic growth in the numbers of unemployed employables receiving social assistance. In the early 1970s, this category of recipients accounted for no more than 10 to 20 percent of the caseload. The vast majority of beneficiaries at the time were either disabled, elderly or single mothers. Although the definitions of "employable" vary significantly across provinces, the numbers for recent years indicate that this category makes up from 30 to close to 80 percent of the caseload. Most provinces are in the 50 to 70 percent range, with British Columbia and Ontario featuring the highest ratios.[55]

The fact that employables now constitute a major part of the social assistance caseload is not expected to change in the near future. A recent study on the growth of government spending[56] identifies the following factors as likely to create pressures on CAP-related programs in the future:

- high unemployment rates, which are not expected to decline rapidly in the coming years even with the end of the recession;

- the positive correlation between high unemployment rates and the duration of unemployment;

- the shift towards more part-time, low-paying, and temporary jobs;

- the growing mismatch between labour force skills and employers' requirements;

- the tightening of accessibility to unemployment insurance benefits; and

- the rapid growth in the number of single parents.

The increase in the number of employables dependent on social assistance has significant implications for the redesign and the financing of CAP programs. First of all, it dramatically increases the strain on programs that were not designed to deal with the problems associated with unemployment. The issues here concern the types of services available (e.g., vocational rehabilitation, training and placement measures to secure employment) and the ability to integrate work incentive measures (e.g., the treatment of earned income when calculating benefits) into the programs. On both these issues the record so far is not good. Services available under CAP to help individuals return to the labour force are either insufficient or inadequate, and the integration of work incentives has been constrained by the needs-test requirement.

The lack of flexibility inherent in CAP in this regard has been apparent for quite some time. One of the main criticisms of CAP in the 1981 Breau Report concerned the needs-test requirement to determine eligibility for social assistance. Needs testing, which involves the specification of asset and income thresholds relative to designated "need," has been a problem for provinces wanting to implement programs of income supplementation for the working poor under CAP. Although needs testing may have been appropriate at a time when the program clientele was not expected to earn income through employment, it has now become a stumbling block in designing programs with built-in incentives to work and measures to escape the welfare trap. Indeed, provinces have either had to incorporate an otherwise unnecessary form of needs testing into their wage supplementation programs (as in Saskatchewan) or maintain an income-tested approach and forego cost-sharing transfers (as in Quebec and Manitoba).[57]

The 1986 report of the Nielsen Task Force on CAP[58] underscored the fact that some of the measures being developed in a number of provinces to reduce CAP caseloads entail expenditures that cannot be cost-shared under CAP provisions but that can have both positive and negative consequences for the federal budget. This illustrates some of the perverse incentives built into the existing programs. For instance, provincial wage supplementation programs for the working poor, in preventing additions to the caseload, translate into implicit savings for the federal government. Provincial make-work projects, on the other hand, can lead to individuals being reintegrated into the workforce or resorting to federal UI benefits following termination of the projects.

It was in order to address some of these inconsistencies that the federal ministers of National Health and Welfare and Employment and Immigration, along with the provincial ministers with responsibility for income security and labour markets, developed, in 1985, a set of special Agreements to Enhance the Employability of Social Assistance Recipients. The current five-year agreement commits up to $400 million annually (with each level of government contributing an equal share) to be spent on training and employment programs to help assistance recipients make the transition to work. However, these initiatives have had to be implemented outside the confines of CAP. Indeed, the programs are supported by funds that would otherwise have been spent on social assistance and, in effect, involve a diversion of CAP funds to other programs.[59]

A further consequence of the greater proportion of employables dependent on welfare is that the demand for social assistance is increasingly tied to the general state of the economy, thereby accentuating the counter-cyclical pattern and the regional incidence differentials described above. Moreover, with continued increases in caseloads expected, the question arises as to whether the resulting costs will be sustainable over time. Already in 1985, the Task Force on Program Review was expressing some concern over the cost implications of these trends: "The Study Team does not consider the cost of CAP excessive relative to its purpose, to other programs and in relation to the severity of the circumstances of the needy in Canada. However, this cost could become unaffordable if present economic trends continue, forcing a change in the open-ended character of funding arrangements."[60]

While CAP had been exempted from federal fiscal restraint measures from its inception until the 1990-91 fiscal year, the 1990 federal budget imposed a five percent annual growth ceiling on total entitlements in any province not eligible for transfers under the fiscal equalization program. The ceiling was initially to be imposed only for a two-year period; however the 1991 federal budget extended its application for a further three years. The province of Ontario has estimated that the three-year loss to the three affected provinces — Ontario, Alberta and British Columbia — will exceed $4 billion, 85 percent of which will be borne directly by Ontario. According to these estimates, Ontario's CAP losses amount to $1.8 billion or 29 percent of the province's operating deficit for 1992-93 alone.[61]

The main effect of the cap on CAP is that, in the three have provinces, CAP no longer operates as a cost-matching program. According to the Ontario estimates, the federal government, in effect, would only be paying for 28 percent of eligible costs in Ontario, 47.4 percent in Alberta and 36.8 percent in British Columbia in 1992-93, compared with the standard 50 percent in the other provinces. For these provinces, transfers received under CAP are now akin to a block grant. For instance, the affected provinces no longer need to report spending by category of eligible expenditures to the CAP administration. It is also interesting to note that Ontario's recently proposed agenda for welfare reform is, to a great extent, a departure from CAP-influenced policies.

Finally, although the federal government continues to share equally the costs of social assistance in the have-not provinces, programs here have also been under strain. To participate in cost sharing under CAP, the provinces must first be in a position to contribute their own share. This ability is, of course, related to fiscal capacity and as mentioned in the previous chapter, the tax effort required in the absence of equalization to generate an additional $1 in revenues varies significantly across provinces. With the growth ceiling on equalization in effect and with social assistance spending rising in all provinces during the recent recession, the have-not provinces have been left in the position of having to finance additional spending on social programs through unequalized tax dollars.

Comprehensive Income Security Reform: Back on the Agenda

Although the inadequacies of CAP have long been recognized by both the federal and provincial governments, the plan remains largely unchanged from its original design. Unlike cost-sharing arrangements in other areas of social policy, most notably health care and post-secondary education, which were converted to block funding with the introduction of EPF in 1977, CAP issues have, time after time, been set aside, in expectation that "something better" was about to come along — that something better being the long-awaited comprehensive reform of income security programs.

Indeed, the effectiveness of the income security system is a concern that dates back more than twenty years. During that period, numerous studies, reviews and proposals have reiterated the need to develop a comprehensive and integrated system as a way to address the problems created by years of piecemeal, incremental reforms to existing programs. More significantly, the reform proposals that have emerged over time are surprisingly consistent in terms of the types of changes recommended. In particular, two underlying concepts are common to all proposals: namely, basic income support (often described as guaranteed annual income) for the needy and wage supplementation for the working poor. Under the systems proposed, social assistance programs take on a lesser, complementary role. For instance, based on the latest assessment of income security, the Macdonald Commission favoured the elimination of several federal programs and measures, including federal contributions to social assistance benefits, and the replacement of these with a "universally available income transfer."[62]

The lack of integration of income security programs has been a problem almost from the time the system was put in place. This was practically inevitable, given the rapid proliferation of federal and provincial programs in the 1960s and early 1970s. In fact, the primary objective of the Social Security Review, launched in 1973 by the Minister of National Health and Welfare,[63] was to examine the possibility of implementing a comprehensive and coordinated income maintenance system. Also at issue was the question of adequate and equitable treatment of the working poor. As a result of this process, it was proposed that a two-tier system be established with income supplements and built-in work incentives provided to those able and expected to work and income support for those unable to work.

The system proposed under the Review was meant to remove the great majority of people from social assistance as we know it. Income support would be provided primarily through a new guaranteed annual income scheme and programs under CAP would be reduced to a residual support role to address special needs.[64] The levels of income guarantees and supplementation would be determined by individual provinces, although Parliament would reserve the right to set minimum benefit levels nationally. In terms of funding arrangements, the proposal called for federal-provincial CAP-type cost matching for the income support component, whereas income supplementation would be financed on the basis of two-thirds federal, one-third provincial cost sharing.[65]

The recommendations also included a social and employment services strategy that involved broadening and enhancing social services provided under CAP, particularly those considered necessary to make the employment and income supplementation strategy more efficient and effective (e.g., training, counselling, placement, rehabilitation and child care services).

Although the proposed reform received wide approval in principle, the recommendations were never implemented. More significantly, the factors that prevented the adoption of the Review's recommendations at the time are the same ones that appear to stand in the way of a comprehensive reform of income security today — namely, the difficulty of determining which level of government should operate the program; the problem of defining appropriate fiscal arrangements; and, perhaps more importantly, concerns over the potential costs involved.[66]

As the income maintenance strategy lost momentum, the proposals regarding social services emerged as the main item on the reform agenda. The Social Services Act (Bill C-57), which was put forth in 1976, called for an expansion of the range and availability of social services. This was to be achieved by eliminating the link between social services delivery and social assistance while maintaining federal-provincial cost matching. The proposal led to a renewed debate as to whether federal cost sharing of social services, a recognized area of provincial jurisdiction, is appropriate. Bill C-57 was therefore withdrawn and replaced by Bill C-55, the Social Services Financing Act, which proposed replacing cost-sharing arrangements for social services under CAP with block funding on a basis similar to the EPF arrangements for health services. Bill C-55 was withdrawn in November 1978 as part of the federal government's efforts to restrain spending.

The Breau Report was equally ambivalent in its recommendations concerning social services. Alternatives under consideration included the continuation of cost-sharing arrangements, the replacement of cost sharing by block funding arrangements akin to EPF, and federal withdrawal with a compensating tax transfer. The debate over the appropriate form of financing for social services stems mainly from two factors: the divergence of views as to the appropriate role of the federal government in this area; and the apparent inconsistency between the range of social services provided and the objectives pursued through these programs.

The CAP's objective in this regard has been to allocate funds to the provinces in order that they can provide welfare services designed to lessen, remove or prevent the causes of poverty and dependence on public assistance.[67] Given this mandate, one would expect social services programs to have emphasized measures aimed at improving the working skills and prospects of disadvantaged individuals. However, as Hum points out in his assessment of CAP services, this has not been the case:

...social services covered under CAP do not focus on skill upgrading, education, job preparation, or job placement, where, perhaps, the potential returns are highest. The element of social investment strategy in the services provided under CAP is in fact minimal and merely "remedial."[68]

Instead, the 20 percent of CAP expenditures for welfare services is mostly allocated to casework, counselling, home support services, rehabilitation, etc. Hum's argument is that these types of services should receive independent standing and not be limited to those individuals defined under CAP as being in "need." In fact, many of these services could be viewed as an extension of health services, particularly in the context of a more comprehensive and preventive approach to health care. This is the reason why previous reform proposals favoured separate funding arrangements for social services.

It is clear, however, that services will be a significant component of any "active" income support strategy. In such a context, a social investment approach to services will be required where the ultimate purpose is to help employable beneficiaries return to the labour market and support themselves. For these types of services, the link between the services and assistance provided needs to be strengthened. Social services could be the key element in developing mechanisms to facilitate the targeting of social assistance benefits and the implementation of appropriate work incentives and employability enhancement programs. The continuing increases in the number of employables on social assistance can only widen the discrepancy between the objectives and outcome of social services currently provided under CAP. This issue will need to be resolved in order to arrive at appropriate fiscal arrangements in this area.

Assessing The Various Options

An assessment of the potential alternatives to the current financing arrangements for social assistance makes it clear that the framework for funding these programs will have to be adapted to the current policy requirements and not the other way around. In addition to the argument that income redistribution is an area of joint constitutional responsibility, there remains the question of whether cost sharing or some other approach is more appropriate in the efficient provision of social assistance in a decentralized system of government.

In its review of CAP, the Breau Report endorsed continued federal-provincial cost sharing for social assistance. In particular, the Task Force supported the view that the federal government has legitimate constitutional jurisdiction with regard to programs of income distribution, including social assistance.[69] The Task Force further argued that this approach ensured the sharing of economic and social risk experienced by any individual region. The open-ended feature of the arrangement was also viewed as appropriate given that provincial assistance costs are directly related to fluctuations in economic circumstances and influenced by the differing regional effects of national economic problems such as unemployment. The Report even went on to suggest that special or enriched cost sharing should be considered for "those portions of the caseload that may be most directly related to economic downturns."[70]

One of the traditional arguments favouring a federal government role through cost-sharing programs has been that individual provinces have an incentive to underspend on benefits to recipients of social assistance for fear of encouraging the immigration of needy individuals from less generous provinces. In the case where individuals care only about their fellow residents, the additional benefits accruing to provincial residents from an additional dollar per-capita in spending on social assistance will be less than those accruing to the country as a whole. Since additional benefits accruing to non-residents are not taken into account in determining levels of provision, this results in underspending by individual provinces on social assistance relative to the best interests of the country as a whole. In order to correct for this source of inefficiency, an appropriate cost-sharing arrangement is called for. Incidentally, there is no presumption that this necessarily requires 50-50 cost sharing.[71]

By their very design, cost-sharing arrangements will alter provincial spending priorities, both in terms of amounts and allocation across programs. Through the effect on relative prices — in this case, by reducing the share of program costs borne by provincial governments — an incentive is provided to increase expenditures in designated program areas. While the provinces have frequently complained that cost-sharing arrangements distort their spending priorities, the spillover argument in the context of social assistance would suggest that maintaining some form of cost sharing is appropriate.

One legitimate claim of the provinces, however, is that conditionality tends to limit the scope for experimentation and innovation in program design and therefore their ability to respond to new circumstances. While it is true that practically any involvement of the federal government will have an influence on provincial spending priorities, it is an undesirable aspect of conditional grant programs that they do not allow provinces sufficient flexibility in program design.

The arguments for continued cost sharing of social services centre mainly on the need for a secure source of funding earmarked for the maintenance and development of services that are still considered "immature." It is generally agreed that, in the area of social services in particular, no semblance of national standards has been achieved. The main arguments against the cost-sharing approach include: concerns about the lack of control over costs; the difficulty, in light of the heterogeneity of social services programs, of setting guidelines as to which programs will be covered; and, finally, the perception of federal interference in an area of recognized provincial jurisdiction.[72]

One of the main problems with the CAP stems from the cost-matching provision and the fact that differences in federal transfers to the provinces may reflect differences in generosity as opposed to differences in need. That the size of CAP transfers to a provinces is determined directly by the level of provincial spending can be seen as favouring wealthier provinces. The have-not provinces have traditionally adopted the position that they are left at a disadvantage under CAP because of their lower fiscal capacity. Because the provinces with greatest need (or welfare burden in terms of number of recipients per capita) tend to be those with the lowest fiscal capacities, they are constrained in their ability to make these expenditures and, therefore, in their ability to participate in cost sharing. For instance, the rate of growth of CAP transfers to the have-not provinces has been markedly slower than that to the have provinces in recent years. According to estimates produced by the Quebec government, transfers under CAP grew by 4.5 percent in the have-not provinces compared to 9.8 percent in the have provinces between 1984-85 and 1990-91.[73] This seems somewhat perverse, particularly because this was also a period of relatively rapid economic growth in the have provinces. Of course, the trend is explained in part by the welfare reforms undertaken in Ontario during this period; but it is also generally a reflection of the wide variations across provinces in need and generosity with respect to social assistance.

Overall, the difficulties associated with cost sharing under CAP are very similar to those that prompted the shift to block funding of established programs (health care and post-secondary education) in 1977. The advantages of such a move also apply in this case. Certainly a federal presence through block funding arrangements can be argued to satisfy constitutional obligations. For example, a block grant made on an equal per-capita basis can be viewed as satisfying federal commitments under section 36 by benefitting those provinces with below-average per-capita expenditure levels (generally speaking the have-not provinces). Moreover, a move to block funding would remove the incentive for provinces to spend more in program areas since the cost of marginal expenditures would be fully borne by provincial treasuries. Thus, the federal government would achieve complete control over its share of program expenditures as these would no longer be tied to provincial spending levels. Finally, block funding would provide provinces with discretion as to the allocation of resources across designated programs, allowing provinces the flexibility to develop social services according to their own priorities.

The policy issues underlying CAP programs, however, are fundamentally different from those related to EPF. CAP involves the financing of income support for needy individuals. It is clear that "need" for social assistance tends to be counter-cyclical; as a consequence, so too will be the need for social services. Thus, a block funding scheme tied to base year per-capita entitlements and escalated in accordance with growth in GDP would seem to be ill-designed in this case. Rather, federal transfers for social assistance and social services ought to be tied to the needs of individual provinces; and certainly these needs would be expected to be inversely related to growth in GDP. Also, relative levels of spending in this area would be expected to change over time for reasons other than population shifts: for example, the relative degree of urbanization or the

differing regional impact of economic restructuring might also be significant determinants. Block funding arrangements generally do not reflect
interprovincial differences in need or cost of delivery. In this respect,
cost-sharing arrangements would appear to be more appropriate.

The option of a withdrawal of federal spending in provincial social
assistance and social services programs, accompanied by a corresponding
transfer of tax room to the provinces, presents many of the same problems. The transfer of tax room would be tied to existing average per-capita
transfers, which are a reflection of existing economic conditions and may
not be appropriate to conditions at other times in the future. Moreover,
the value of the tax transfer would grow with the tax base — that is,
inversely to growth in social assistance spending. Nor would a tax transfer
reflect changes in relative economic circumstances among provinces.
Finally, while transferred tax points would be eligible for fiscal equalization, the have-not provinces would be left at a disadvantage since the
equalized value would, under the existing formula, be less than the
national average yield. This problem is made even more acute by the
presence of the growth ceiling on equalization entitlements. Thus, the
design of an appropriate tax transfer would require an ongoing commitment of federal funds to levelling and transitional payments if the option
were to receive provincial support.

Proposal For Renewed Cost Sharing

The issues underlying CAP and the programs financed under the plan can
only be addressed in the context of the federal-provincial entanglement
in the income security field. This entanglement is directly related to the
fact that both levels of government have joint responsibility in the area of
income distribution. Based on the arguments presented, we believe that
there is a strong case for maintaining cost-sharing arrangements in the
social assistance and social services areas on both constitutional and economic grounds. We are, however, sensitive to federal concerns over
expenditure control as well as transparency and accountability issues. In
fact, our proposal is founded on the principles of fiscal equalization, but
with an emphasis on interprovincial equalization in respect of social
assistance liabilities.

More specifically, we propose a new cost-sharing scheme where the total federal contribution is based on a fixed percentage of standard social assistance expenditure per capita but where the level of payments to individual provinces varies to take into account differences in relative welfare burdens across provinces. The basis for our proposal is the recognition that income transfers through social assistance are equivalent to negative taxes. Put another way, if social assistance were delivered entirely through some form of refundable tax credit it would be buried within the provincial income tax system and reflected in provincial income tax revenues.[74] Since relatively high welfare burdens result in higher social-assistance transfers (negative taxes), these should be reflected in measures of fiscal capacity. Moreover, differences in welfare burdens affect the provinces' abilities to provide comparable services at comparable levels of taxation. The argument relates back to the notion of differential NFBs across provinces referred to in chapter 2. In this light, there is a case for applying the principles of fiscal equalization to social assistance expenditures.[75]

The actual formula for calculating entitlements for social assistance equalization would be similar to that used for fiscal equalization. A province's entitlement would be based on the difference between its own per-capita liability for social assistance and the national average. The notion of social assistance liability parallels that of fiscal capacity. Instead of assessing provinces' relative ability to raise revenues under a Representative Tax System, the objective is to compare provinces' relative social assistance burdens under a "Representative Benefit System" (RBS). This is done by multiplying a given province's standardized (i.e., eligible) number of recipients per capita by a standardized benefits level per recipient and comparing the results with the corresponding national average. Thus, the standardized benefits level per recipient corresponds to the national average tax rates used in the equalization formula while the standardized number of recipients per capita corresponds to the per-capita tax bases.

Using this approach would require defining a common set of eligibility criteria for social assistance and a common level of benefits per recipient for the purposes of comparing provincial liabilities under social assistance, which we have termed the RBS. The standard benefit level could be tied to the national average, or limits could be placed on allowable benefits. It could even reflect cost-of-living differentials across provinces.

The appropriate eligibility criteria and standard benefits levels making up the RBS would need to be determined jointly by the federal government and the provinces.

Notice that a province's standardized per-capita social assistance liability could be interpreted as a measure of "need" for social assistance spending. What the equalization formula does, then, is to allow us to calculate entitlements based on relative provincial "need." Such a system effectively equalizes for differences in need for social assistance; those provinces with above-average need would have positive entitlements, those with below-average need would have negative entitlements.

In our view, it is likely to be politically unacceptable to attempt to incorporate social assistance liabilities into the existing equalization program. Provinces receive equalization transfers only when their overall fiscal capacity is lower than the five-province standard. If social assistance liabilities were incorporated into the fiscal equalization program, some provinces with above-average social-assistance need might not be eligible for transfers once all the categories covered under equalization were tallied. In other words, provinces with net positive entitlements for social assistance needs would only receive equalization if their overall entitlements for fiscal equalization were positive.[76] As a result, the have provinces, which are currently eligible for payments under CAP, would no longer receive federal contributions to cover part of their social assistance liabilities.

Our recommendation is that the system be operated parallel to the fiscal equalization program through a modified federal-provincial cost-sharing scheme. The total federal commitment to cost sharing would be a fixed percentage, say 50 percent, of standardized provincial social assistance liabilities. Each province's per-capita entitlement, then, would be calculated as 50 percent of standardized national per-capita liability plus an equalization amount determined by the difference between its standardized per-capita liability and the corresponding national average. This amount would, of course, be positive or negative depending on whether the province exhibits above- or below-average liability (need). The built-in equalization factor, therefore, results in a system of differential cost sharing where provinces with above-average need would receive greater than 50 percent cost sharing, and those with below-average need would receive less than 50 percent cost sharing.

In symbols, the formula for calculating each province's social assistance transfer would be:

$$S_i = .5b_i r_c N_i + b_i[r_i - r_c]N_i$$

where $\quad S_i$ = social assistance transfer to province i

b_i = standardized benefits per recipient in province i

r_c = standardized national recipients per capita

N_i = province i's population

r_i = standardized recipients per capita in province i

Our proposal is equivalent, in effect, to a block grant, equalized for differences in social assistance liabilities. This could be replicated through an equal per-capita revenue transfer accompanied by an equalization scheme as described above — in effect an inter-provincial revenue-pooling scheme. The advantage of our proposal, however, is that the equalization component is administered directly by the federal government, a feature we see as being central to the sustainability of a revenue-pooling system such as this.

Such an arrangement, because it is tied to standardized expenditure levels, would significantly reduce the ability of individual provinces to increase the size of their grant, eliminating the "incentive to spend" problem associated with cost matching. At the same time, the scheme would maintain the federal commitment to the principle of cost sharing. Provinces would continue to have complete discretion in setting their own eligibility requirements and benefits levels; where these are in excess of the limits used in the formula, additional expenditures would have to be funded out of provincial revenues. In addition, the implicit escalator for social assistance transfers would be annual growth in standard provincial expenditures and would thus reflect the counter-cyclical nature of social assistance expenditures (unlike, for example, growth in GDP). Finally, the equalization factor takes into account differences in economic circumstances across provinces and, because the system operates separately from the fiscal equalization program, it would allow non-recipient provinces under fiscal equalization to benefit as well from a higher degree of cost sharing during years in which provincial need for social assistance is above the national average. Thus, the formula conforms with the notion of risk sharing, both economic and social, that has characterized Canadian federalism.

five

toward sustainable fiscal federalism

Existing federal-provincial fiscal arrangements should be viewed in their historical context, as a link in the evolution of fiscal federalism in Canada. Each element of these arrangements has its own particular history and its own distinct role to play. Taken as a whole, however, the fiscal arrangements have served the federation well in promoting the dual goals of fiscal equity and economic efficiency in what is a highly decentralized federal system of government. The pressures of rising deficits and crippling debt have created an environment in which the fiscal arrangements will now inevitably undergo a further step in their evolution. Reform is long overdue.

A central feature of the practice of fiscal federalism in Canada has been the dominant role played by the federal government in the personal and corporate income tax fields. Among other things, this has allowed the federal government to maintain a significant presence in provincial finances through the major fiscal transfer programs — Equalization, EPF and CAP. We have argued, however, that various *ad hoc* modifications to these programs in recent years have seriously compromised the important redistributive function of the federal government, to the detriment of both fiscal equity and economic efficiency. In particular, these measures have left all provinces scrambling to make up shortfalls in revenues under the major transfers in order to maintain social programs. This has been especially the case for the have-not provinces, whose own-source fiscal capacities are significantly below the national average. Such a trend has serious implications for the continuing ability of provinces to finance comparable levels of public services at comparable levels of taxation, and thus threatens the concept of "national" social programs. As a consequence, a key principle of Canadian federalism is now in serious jeopardy. Failure to recognize and address this issue raises the spectre of a crisis for federalism in Canada unprecedented since Confederation.

Specifically, the have-not provinces' ability to fund rapidly rising expenditures in health, education and welfare has deteriorated significantly (as a direct consequence of the growth ceiling on equalization entitlements and the freeze on EPF entitlements) relative to the have provinces. In addition, federal budget measures that discriminate against the have provinces (in particular, the cap on CAP) have not only strained the fiscal positions of those provinces, but has put into question the future of cost-sharing arrangements and, more fundamentally, the role of the federal government in financing provincial social assistance expenditures.

Ultimately, the issue boils down to the division of income tax room between the federal government and the provinces.[77] The post-war development of Canada's "national" social programs was initially fuelled by the use of the federal spending power through a variety of cost-sharing programs established in the fields of post-secondary education, health care and welfare. These transfers were, in part, provided in lieu of the return to the provinces of income tax room ceded under the wartime Tax Rental Agreements. With the introduction of EPF, the growth in per-capita federal transfers to the provinces in respect of post-secondary education and health care was thereafter to be tied directly to growth in per-capita GDP under a new block-funding scheme. Transfers in respect of provincial welfare programs under CAP, on the other hand, remained on an open-ended cost-matching basis until 1990, at which time a five percent annual growth ceiling was placed on entitlements in each of the have provinces.

EPF: The Next Step

We have interpreted EPF as a program under which the federal government effectively provided the provinces with a fully equalized transfer of income tax room in respect of health care and post-secondary education expenditures. By this, we refer to the number of tax points that would have yielded the equivalent value of revenues actually transferred to the provinces through the combination of cash and tax transfers under EPF in 1977. This effective "transfer" of tax room was fully equalized in the sense that the net result was an equal per-capita revenue yield to the provinces.

Unlike in earlier transfers of tax room, however, the effective number of tax points "transferred" under EPF has become progressively smaller over time. This is a result both of the design of the program and of a series of federal expenditure control measures that have constrained the growth of entitlements compared with the growth in the value of the associated tax points.[78] Thus, it might be argued that the federal government has been unilaterally pre-empting income tax room that had been effectively "transferred" to the provinces under EPF.

The five-year freeze on per-capita EPF entitlements introduced in the 1990 federal budget has further strained the program by causing a precipitous erosion in the cash component of the transfer.[79] This has two immediate consequences. First, it further erodes federal leverage over the provinces aimed at maintaining the principles of the Canada Health Act in the delivery of health care programs. There is considerable question and controversy over the national standards issue, much of it overstated. Nevertheless, whatever the merits of the conflicting views, the suggestion by the federal government that it could maintain its leverage over provinces in the health care field by withholding non-health transfers poses potential problems. Such withholding could, for example, compromise the attainment of the various objectives attached to other programs. Second, the freeze on EPF may lead to a situation in which cash entitlements are, in fact, negative. Unless these negative cash entitlements are recovered from the provinces, EPF entitlements will no longer operate as an equal per-capita transfer: the fully equalized nature of the effective tax transfer will be gone. Rather, per-capita EPF entitlements will become greater in those provinces with relatively greater fiscal capacities. Moreover, since the EPF transfer will ultimately be delivered entirely through the tax component, in effect there will be no more transfer: EPF will be defunct as an element of federal-provincial fiscal transfers.

Thus, we have adopted the view that the transfer of tax points under EPF remains as unfinished business on the federal-provincial fiscal relations agenda. In order to preserve the equivalence between the total per-capita EPF transfer and a fully equalized transfer of tax room, we have argued that the existing total cash transfer to the provinces under EPF should be converted to a tax abatement, whereby a fixed percentage of federal income tax revenues would be earmarked for EPF. These revenues would form a pool from which the per-capita value of the existing EPF tax points (including any associated equalization) by province would be raised to a "top-province" standard. The balance of the pool would then be distributed across provinces on an equal per-capita basis. This would accomplish a complete fiscal disentanglement in funding programs included under EPF (the federal government would simply be collecting revenues on behalf of the provinces) and would halt the erosion in the implicit number of EPF tax points. Thereafter, the value of the tax abatement would vary directly with federal income tax revenues.

By adopting the tax abatement approach rather than providing the provinces with a direct transfer of tax room, the federal government maintains the responsibility for redistributing revenues on behalf of the provinces. Such an approach, in effect a form of inter-provincial revenue sharing, would be a significant new direction in Canadian fiscal federalism, signifying a renewed commitment to the sharing community.

CAP: Redefining Roles

Historically, the role of the provinces in welfare has been to administer to the needs of those deemed unemployable. Increasingly, however, responsibility for unemployed employables has been shifted to the provinces. The most recent example of this can be found in the new restrictions in UI rules announced in the 1993 federal budget, which will inevitably result in increases in the provincial welfare rolls. In addition, a period of protracted recession has itself swollen provincial caseloads. At the same time, the federal government has lessened its commitment to cost sharing under the CAP by limiting growth in entitlements in the have provinces. The have-not provinces have also been left lame in their capacity to cope with rising welfare burdens as a consequence of the growth ceiling on aggregate equalization entitlements.

It is clear that a major and comprehensive overhaul of the income security system is long overdue and that an important aspect of this will be a recasting of the role of social assistance. Whether governments are prepared to extend some form of guaranteed annual income to those unable or not expected to work, as has often been recommended in the past, remains to be seen. It nonetheless seems clear that the number of unemployed employables requiring income support will remain significant in the current economic climate. We assume that unemployment insurance will continue to be a federal area of responsibility and that any changes to this program would be in line with proposals put forward in numerous studies on the subject. Thus, we assume that any reform of UI will be consistent with social insurance principles, with less emphasis on responding to specific sectoral or regional circumstances. This has obvious consequences both in terms of the need for social assistance and the importance of integrated and preventive measures within the system. In this context, wage supplementation, built-in work incentives and employability enhancement measures become paramount. For these and other reasons, we do not believe a withdrawal of federal spending in provincial social assistance and social services programs is justified. Moreover, we maintain that there should be a broader definition of the types of programs that would be included under cost-sharing arrangements.

In previous reform proposals, it has been argued that separate funding arrangements could be developed for social services. We do not agree. To separate funding arrangements for social assistance from those for social services is to ignore the complementary nature of the programs involved. In fact, the links need to be strengthened. Social services will be instrumental in the implementation of any "active" income support strategy, in particular in the targeting of benefits and the implementation of appropriate work incentives and employability enhancement programs.

It is our view that a new cost-sharing scheme can be devised to overcome the main deficiencies of CAP while maintaining its positive features. We have argued that income transfers to individuals through social assistance are equivalent to negative taxes and, as such, should be reflected in measurements of provincial fiscal capacities. Our proposal for reforming CAP is founded on the principles of fiscal equalization: however, we place on the provinces, rather than on the federal government, the onus for equalization in respect of social assistance liabilities.

Under our proposed scheme, the total federal commitment would be based on a fixed percentage of standard social assistance expenditures per capita. For a given level of benefits per recipient, the total federal commitment would vary inversely with the national economic cycle, rising or falling with the average number of recipients per capita. Each province's per-capita entitlement would be adjusted via a built-in equalization factor designed to reflect the difference between its per-capita social assistance liability and the corresponding national average. This amount would be positive or negative depending on whether the province exhibits above- or below-average "need." The net effect of this would be that provinces with above-average need would receive a larger per-capita transfer for social assistance than those with below-average need. This would mean that, in the case where the federal share in funding provincial social assistance expenditures is, say, 50 percent, those provinces with above-average need would be eligible for greater than 50 percent cost sharing, while those with below-average need would be eligible for less than 50 percent cost sharing. This results from fully equalizing differences between provincial per-capita liabilities and the corresponding national average.

A significant aspect of the equalization component of this scheme is that it would require no further commitment of revenues by the federal government; rather, equalization would be achieved through *de facto* interprovincial revenue pooling. It should also be noted that all provinces would be treated equally under the formula, receiving a positive equalization adjustment in periods of above-average liability for social assistance and a negative equalization adjustment in periods of below-average liability. Thus, not only does the formula promote fiscal equity and efficiency, it also conforms nicely to the "insurance" principle of federalism.

The Sharing Community: A New Orientation

While the issues underlying EPF and CAP may be fundamentally different, there is in our proposals a common thread: if the provinces wish to attain greater control over their own fiscal destinies, they must first be prepared to undertake a commitment to interprovincial revenue sharing. In other words, the provinces themselves must be willing to play a more direct role in promoting the dual goals of fiscal equity and economic efficiency in the

Canadian federation. Our proposals amount to a clearer definition of how revenues are to be shared between the federal and provincial governments with respect to funding social programs. Each of our proposed schemes incorporates an element of internal equalization. In contrast with the existing fiscal equalization program, however, they operate on a net basis. It should be noted, finally, that a key role is identified for the federal government in our proposed reforms: the sustainability of the proposed arrangements depends on federal coordination of the equalization components.

Adopting these proposals would, in our view, go a long way towards eliminating the tensions that have surfaced in Canadian fiscal federalism over the past number of years. To a large extent, these tensions appear to be a response to federal budget measures that are tantamount to a unilateral federal pre-emption of tax room in respect of EPF and CAP. For this reason, the western provinces have called for a "fully equalized" transfer of tax room as a means of achieving fiscal disentanglement. Similarly, Ontario has forcefully argued that the shortfall in cash transfers under EPF and CAP has been a principal cause of the province's ballooning deficit, and is now demanding its "share" of federal tax dollars.

From the perspective of the have-not provinces, the situation is even grimmer. It has been exacerbated by the impact of the growth ceiling imposed on fiscal equalization. The have-not provinces are having to cope with revenue shortfalls under EPF as well as rising welfare expenditures due to the effects of the recession. These shortfalls threaten to open up significant gaps in provinces' abilities to provide comparable levels of public services at comparable levels of taxation, since the provinces are having to compensate through own-source revenues but with significant differences in fiscal capacities.

Canadian fiscal federalism is indeed at a critical point in its evolution. While we do not dispute the need for both levels of government to address their debt and deficit problems, it must be recognized that the *ad hoc* measures adopted with respect to the major fiscal transfer programs have seriously weakened the foundations of the entire system. This has given rise to a redistributional backlash in the have provinces. So far, at least, their concerns appear to have more to do with the federal government's penchant for unilaterally altering the fiscal arrangements in respect of social programs than with any weakening of commitment to the principle of redistribution *per se.* The have provinces are simply demanding a more predictable and equitable approach to federal-provincial revenue sharing. But the danger signs are there. If their concerns are not met, the have provinces will intensify calls for a direct transfer of income tax room, placing in jeopardy the central role of the federal government in effecting interprovincial redistribution.

Sustainable fiscal federalism in Canada will require a clearer definition of the division of income tax room between the federal government and the provinces in respect of social programs. On this issue, we differ completely from those who would simply scrap EPF and CAP, with or without a transfer of tax points to the provinces, and rely on fiscal equalization, perhaps enriched, to cushion the impact on the have-not provinces. Fiscal equalization alone cannot sustain and extend the enviable record of the Canadian model of fiscal federalism in promoting the dual goals of fiscal equity and economic efficiency. Rather than radically reforming the practice of fiscal equalization, a system that works relatively well in its present form, our preference is for reforming EPF and CAP in such a way as to enhance their complementary role in promoting fiscal equity and economic efficiency. In our view, a clearer definition of revenue sharing would leave the provinces in a better position to undertake much-needed reforms in the area of social policy.

Notes

1. A theme developed by Richard Simeon in "The Political Context For Renegotiating Fiscal Federalism," a paper presented at the Conference on The Future of Fiscal Federalism, Queen's University, November 4, 1993 (mimeo.), pp. 10-12.

2. After the failure of the Charlottetown Accord, some observers have argued that, due to their overall implications, negotiations on the fiscal arrangements may constitute, in effect, the next constitutional round.

3. Ontario, Ministry of Treasury and Economics, *1992 Budget, Meeting Ontario's Priorities* (Toronto: Queen's Printer for Ontario, 1992), Budget Paper D, p. 101.

4. The situation is actually reversed for the current fiscal year. With all the provinces facing declining income tax revenues as a result of the latest recession, equalization entitlements are down; and, because of the decline in value of EPF tax points, the residual cash transfers under EPF have increased. A return to normal growth in tax revenues will result in a situation closer to that described in the text.

5. Report of the Western Finance Ministers, *Economic and Fiscal Development and Federal-Provincial Fiscal Relations in Canada* (Lloydminster, Saskatchewan, 1990), p. 20.

6. See Canada, *Consensus Report on the Constitution: Final Text*, Charlottetown, August 28, 1992.

7. Break describes intergovernmental transfer programs as the basis of a fiscal partnership between two levels of government which develop as either joint ventures or uneasy alliances. See George F. Break, *Financing Government in a Federal System* (Washington: The Brookings Institution, 1980), p. 87.

8. We refer to efficiency in service delivery.

9. This phrase is borrowed from Peter M. Leslie, "The Fiscal Crisis of Canadian Federalism" in Peter M. Leslie, Kenneth Norrie and Irene Ip, *A Partnership in Trouble: Renegotiating Fiscal Federalism* (Toronto: C. D. Howe Institute, 1983), p. 1.

10. Robin Boadway, "Renewing Fiscal Federalism," *Policy Options*, Vol. 14, no. 10 (December 1993), pp. 4-8.

11. We are assuming that the federal fiscal system otherwise confers uniform NFBs on individuals who are equally well off regardless of province of residence.

12. The equilibrium point at which further productivity increases could not be attained through a reallocation of labour across provinces.

13. Parliamentary Task Force on Federal-Provincial Fiscal Arrangements, *Fiscal Federalism in Canada* (Ottawa: Minister of Supply and Services, 1981), pp. 31-32.

14. Conseil économique du Canada, *Un projet commun: Aspects économiques des choix constitutionnels, vingt-huitième Exposé annuel* (Ottawa: Ministre des Approvisionnements et Services, 1991), pp. 67-68.

15. Similar conclusions are also reached in a recent paper by Ruggeri, Howard and Van Wart. See, G.C. Ruggeri, R. Howard and D. Van Wart, "Structural Imbalances in the Canadian Fiscal System," *Canadian Tax Journal*, Vol. 41, no. 3 (August 1993), pp. 454-472.

16. Allan Maslove, "Reconstructing Fiscal Federalism" in Francis Abele (ed.), *How Ottawa Spends: The Politics of Competitiveness, 1992-93* (Ottawa: Carleton University Press, 1992), p. 61.

17. It should be noted, too, that the economics literature is by no means conclusive as to whether a lack of direct accountability will necessarily give rise to inefficient decision making by lower levels of government. Much hinges on the extent to which governments take into account in their budgetary decision the potential migration response of individuals.

18. See *1992 Budget, Meeting Ontario's Priorities*, p. 109.

19. See Robin W. Boadway and Paul A. R. Hobson, *Intergovernmental Fiscal Relations in Canada* (Toronto: Canadian Tax Foundation, 1993), p. 121.

20. For a more detailed description of these events see *Fiscal Federalism in Canada*, pp. 37-41.

21. See *Fiscal Federalism in Canada*, p. 39.

22. A tax abatement is different from a transfer of tax points in that the federal government makes tax room available by a special deduction after the federal basic tax is determined.

23. See *1992 Budget, Meeting Ontario's Priorities*, p. 107.

24. See Quebec, Ministry of Finance, *Budget Papers 1991-1992, Budget Speech and Additional Information* (Quebec: Ministry of Finance, 1992), appendix E, p. 10.

25. See Quebec, *Budget Papers 1991-1992*, appendix E, p. 9.

26. Under Bill C-20, which received Royal Assent in December 1991, Ottawa is able to withhold funds owed to a province under other programs if EPF cash payments do not cover the dollar-for-dollar withholding called for by the Canada Health Care Act in cases where extra-billing and/or user fees have been permitted.

27. Quebec is an exception here due to the additional tax abatement, the value of which is included in calculating the cash transfer.

28. The shift in 1982 to a residual cash component under EPF was particularly important in light of the change to the equalization standard from the national average to the representative five-province standard. Had the original (1977) program design for EPF remained in place, the equalized value of the tax transfer would have fallen below the national average in the have-not provinces without any compensation through the basic cash transfer, thus discriminating against the have-not provinces. This potential problem was resolved by adjusting the program such that the cash component became a residual amount.

29. We will ignore the allocation between personal and corporate income taxes since it does not materially affect our argument. One should note that full equalization requires voluntary interprovincial revenue pooling and equal per-capita distribution.

30. This is, of course, an extension of the argument made by the provinces that the federal government has been unilaterally reducing cash transfers.

31. This would appear to lend some definition to the notion of transferring "fully equalized tax room" in place of EPF cash contained in the Western Finance Ministers Report, *Economic and Fiscal Development*.

32. Boadway and Hobson (In *Intergovernmental Fiscal Relations*) go further than this. They argue that one way of attaining fully equalized fiscal capacities would be to compute EPF entitlements as a net entitlement; that is, actual entitlement plus equalization entitlement. For those provinces with negative equalization entitlement (the have provinces), then, the net EPF entitlement would be less than for the have-not provinces. Under such a scheme, the net effect would be to equalize fully the per-capita revenues of the provinces. While this would be consistent with the equity and efficiency arguments presented in The Economic Council, *Financing Confederation: Today and Tomorrow* (Ottawa: Minister of Supply and Services, 1982), it would involve a significantly expanded federal presence in cash transfers. Certainly the levels of cash transfers under EPF at present would be insufficient to achieve this goal.

33. See *Fiscal Federalism in Canada*, p. 147.

34. See Maslove, "Reconstructing Fiscal Federalism," p. 61.

35. This has been acknowledged by the federal government. See Canada, Department of Finance, *The Budget, February 26, 1991* (Ottawa: Department of Finance, 1991), p. 63.

36. Gallup Canada, *The Gallup Report*, Toronto, August 1, 1991.

37. See Maslove, "Reconstructing Fiscal Federalism," pp. 57-77.

38. See Thomas J. Courchene, *Social Policy in the 1990s* (Toronto: C.D. Howe Institute, 1987), pp. 139-148.

39. Carolyn Tuohy, "Health Policy and Fiscal Federalism," a paper delivered at the Conference on The Future of Fiscal Federalism, Queen's University, November 5, 1993 (mimeo.), p. 15. According to Tuohy, the similarities of interests of the medical profession across provinces have been and will continue to be a significant factor in limiting variations in provincial systems.

40. As has been pointed out by Maslove and others, the fact that there are no explicit national standards for post-secondary education has not prevented a "national" system to evolve in this area without federal intervention.

41. The latest comprehensive review of income security in Canada was that of the Macdonald

Commission. See Royal Commission on the Economic Union and Development Prospects for Canada, *Report,* Vol. 2 (Ottawa: Minister of Supply and Services,1985), pp. 769-802. However, very similar views and concerns were expressed in the context of the Social Security Review as early as 1973.

42. A term taken from Canada, National Council of Welfare, *Welfare in Canada: The Tangled Safety Net* (Ottawa: Minister of Supply and Services, 1987).

43. Royal Commission on Dominion-Provincial Relations, *Report,* Vol. 2 (Ottawa: King's Printer, 1939), p. 24.

44. Historically, provinces had delegated responsibility for welfare to local governments. In recent years, provincial governments have taken a more dominant role, although some welfare programs are still administered at the local level, for example in Ontario and Nova Scotia.

45. For a thorough analysis of these issues see Jonathan Kesselman, "Income Security Via the Tax System: Canadian and American Reforms," in J.B. Shoven and J. Whalley (eds.), *Canada-U.S. Tax Comparisons* (Chicago: The University of Chicago Press, 1992), pp. 97-150.

46. Tax expenditure estimates for 1988 and 1989 are reported in Canada, Department of Finance, *Government of Canada Personal Income Tax Expenditures* (Ottawa: Department of Finance, December 1992), pp. 11-14.

47. Low-income tax reductions allow provinces to eliminate provincial tax liability for individuals with incomes below a specified level and, above this level, to phase in liability over a given range of incomes until the provincial rate applies. Refundable, income-tested sales and property tax credits are provided in Ontario and Manitoba. British Columbia has an income-tested non-refundable credit for rental payments. In recent years Manitoba, Saskatchewan and Alberta have experimented with flat taxes in addition to taxes levied against basic federal tax. Discretionary provincial tax credits create yet another issue. For example, the Ontario property tax credit is currently not cost-shared but housing subsidies provided through social services are. It could be argued that in order to provide provinces

with the appropriate incentive to undertake innovation and experimentation in the delivery of social assistance, transfers effected through the tax system should be treated symmetrically with cash transfers for purposes of cost sharing.

48. Quebec administers its own personal income tax. As well, this does not apply in the case of refundable tax credits since these are calculated independently of the basic federal tax to which provincial tax rates are applied.

49. The acronym APPORT stands for *Aide aux parents pour leurs revenus de travail.*

50. See for example, Western Finance Ministers, *Report of the Western Finance Ministers: Supplement,* August, 1990.

51. Canada, Department of Finance, *Personal Income Tax Coordination: The Federal-Provincial Tax Collection Agreements* (Ottawa:Department of Finance, 1991).

52. Allan Moscovitch, "The Canada Assistance Plan: A Twenty Year Assessment, 1966-1986," in Katherine A. Graham (ed.), *How Ottawa Spends* (Ottawa: Carleton University Press, 1988), p. 285.

53. For a description of the differences in rules and procedures and various benefit levels across provinces, see National Council of Welfare, *Welfare Incomes 1992* (Ottawa: Minister of Supply and Services, 1993).

54. The interaction between CAP programs and other income security programs is described further in Canada, Task Force on Program Review, *Canada Assistance Plan: A Study Team Report to the Task Force on Program Review* (Ottawa: Minister of Supply and Services, 1986), pp. 15-18.

55. This observation is based on unpublished data provided by the Social Program Information Division of Health and Welfare Canada.

56. Canada, Department of Finance, *Federal-Provincial Study on the Cost of Government and Expenditure Management* (Ottawa: Department of Finance, 1992), p. 157.

57. Also see Derek Hum, *Federalism and the Poor: A Review of the Canada Assistance Plan* (Toronto: Ontario Economic Council, 1983), p. 67.

58. See Task Force on Program Review, *Canada Assistance Plan,* 1986.

59. Moscovitch, "The Canada Assistance Plan", p. 295.

60. Task Force on Program Review, *Canada Assistance Plan,* p. 14.

61. See *1992 Budget, Meeting Ontario's Priorities,* p. 103.

62. See Royal Commission on the Economic Union, Vol. 2, pp. 794-801.

63. Canada, National Health and Welfare, *Working Paper on Social Security in Canada,* 2nd ed. (Ottawa: Minister of Health and Welfare, 1973). This paper was to be used as a basis of discussion in the context of a federal-provincial conference of welfare ministers.

64. Canada, Health and Welfare, *Working Paper on Social Security,* p. 34.

65. According to the report of the Parliamentary Task Force on Federal-Provincial Fiscal Arrangements *(Fiscal Federalism in Canada),* programs of income redistribution have traditionally been considered co-jurisdictional, so that the cost-sharing proposal was not seen as using federal spending power in an area of federal jurisdiction (see p. 49). However, some provinces, notably Quebec, have long disagreed with such an interpretation. Also, see Task Force on Program Review, *Canada Assistance Plan,* for further detail on these events.

66. The main outcome on the income maintenance front was the federal Refundable Child Tax Credit, which was introduced in 1978. In addition, some of the more specific suggestions to improve work incentives under CAP were implemented. These included changes in earnings and assets exemptions and clearer guidelines concerning the boundaries for cost sharing.

67. Canada, National Health and Welfare, *Canada Assistance Plan: Annual Report 1991-1992* (Ottawa: Minister of Supply and Services, 1993), p. 9.

68. Hum, *Federalism and the Poor,* p. 72.

69. It could be argued that this view has been reinforced with the enshrinement of the Charter of Rights and Freedoms and section 36 in the Constitution Act, 1982.

70. *Fiscal Federalism in Canada,* p. 144.

71. See Boadway and Hobson, *Intergovernmental Fiscal Relations,* p. 97.

72. This has not been an issue in the case of social assistance, where the federal government is commonly considered to have a role in the context of income redistribution.

73. Quebec, *Budget Papers 1991-1992,* appendix E, p. 22.

74. Thus, reductions in social assistance benefits can be seen as equivalent to increases in personal taxes.

75. See Boadway and Hobson, *Intergovernmental Fiscal Relations,* p. 121.

76. This criticism also applies to the proposal by Boadway and Flatters that entitlements under the three major transfer programs be integrated and paid on a net basis. See Robin Boadway and Frank Flatters "Fiscal Federalism: Is the System in Crisis?", a paper presented at the Conference on the Future of Fiscal Federalism, Queen's University, November 4, 1993 (mimeo.).

77. The introduction of the Goods and Services Tax in 1990 also raised the issue of the division of sales tax room at the retail level between the federal government and those provinces that levy retail sales taxes. As well, the revenue-generating potential of the GST may result in a significant shift in the shares represented by income and sales taxation respectively in total federal revenues. Finally, it can be argued that social programs ought to be financed through a progressive revenue source such as the personal income tax.

78. As explained in chapter 3, this results from the progressive rate structure associated with the personal income tax. To the extent that the income tax base grows proportionately with GDP, a progressive rate structure implies that income tax revenues will grow at a faster rate than GDP.

79. The effect of the latest recession on provincial income tax revenues has put a halt to this trend. In fact, as a result of the decline in provincial income tax revenues, EPF cash transfers are increased for the 1993-94 fiscal year. However, the erosion of the cash transfer will resume as the recovery takes hold.

list of tables and figures

a note on the authors

Paul Hobson is Associate Professor of Economics at Acadia University and a Senior Fellow at IRPP. He has written and researched on fiscal federalism and local public finance and recently co-authored a book entitled *Intergovernmental Fiscal Relations in Canada* (with Robin Boadway), published by the Canadian Tax Foundation.

France St-Hilaire is a Research Director at IRPP. She has researched and written on Canadian public policy, public finance and tax policy. She has previously worked as a researcher at the University of Western Ontario and the University of Toronto, and as an economic consultant.

DATE DUE